# Bruise

Heather Anne

# DEDICATION

For my beautiful Aunt Chelle, high in the heavens. You are my sunshine.

# ACKNOWLEDGMENT

Thanks to everyone on my publishing team for their guidance and assistance in bringing my vision to life.

To my family for their support and suggestions during this process. I appreciate you all more than words can say.

Special thanks to the gorgeous man I'm so lucky to call mine, Terry. Your charm, passion, and unconditional love was the inspiration for the character Weston. Country strong with a heart of gold, you are my eternal "cowboy."

# CONTENTS


Dedication iii

Acknowledgment iv

About the Author vii

Chapter 1 1

Chapter 2 11

Chapter 3 22

Chapter 4 31

Chapter 5 41

Chapter 6 50

Chapter 7 60

Chapter 8 69

Chapter 9 79

Chapter 10 89

Chapter 11 98

Chapter 12 106

Chapter 13 115

Chapter 14 125

Chapter 15 135

Chapter 16 146

Chapter 17      155

Chapter 18      164

Chapter 19      172

Chapter 20      184

Chapter 21      194

# ABOUT THE AUTHOR

Heather currently resides in Central Illinois, nestled in a small farm town with her boys and the love of her life. Inspired by her own trials and tribulations that led her from heartbreak to happiness, she brings you the first in a series of provocative thrillers. Designed to intrigue, excite, and inspire the reader to follow their heart.

Page Blank Intentionally

# CHAPTER 1

Another night in the back of his 1996 F-150, gazing at a sea of shimmering stars. Sitting under the immense glow of the summer sky in the country was like nothing else. The stars were always so bright and vibrant, seemingly endless as they stretched for miles over the fields. It was June in the south, and although it had been uncomfortably hot that day, the evening breeze cut through the humidity like a knife. Snuggled up on the tailgate, he was wearing his favorite Carhartt hoodie and drinking peach moonshine. It was a pretty typical Saturday night for us. Parked out by his mama's pond deep in the backwoods. There, I sat with my high school sweetheart. It seems like a chorus ripped right from a country song on the billboard charts. It was no song, though. It was my reality. My life.

Bonfires with friends were a typical Tuesday. Fridays were meant to be spent under the lights at the football field, and on Sundays, we all still gathered at Grandma's for country-fried steak and her famous crumbled apple cobbler. I was born and raised a country girl in Versailles, Kentucky. Surrounded by loving friends and family, I couldn't have asked for anything more. I grew up riding horses, shooting guns, and racing dirt bikes with the town boys. I was little, blonde, and feisty. I loved my town and upbringing, but I was ready for new scenery and new opportunities. Big city opportunities. I was trading farm life for the fashion industry and was so excited for my future. I collected glamor magazines for years. I had stacks of Vogue, Vanity Fair, Cosmopolitan, and more. I spent hours and, ultimately, years scanning the pages. Observing the beauty and art, creativity and style. I loved it all. It was nothing that was available locally, nothing we even had access to around here. I read every article, learning about the industry and staying current on trends and styles. Even the ads captivated me, the models, the designers, and the sensual fragrances that leaped off the pages. I couldn't wait to be a part of it. My dreams were as tall as the skyscrapers where I was headed. I was going off to learn about fashion and arts, trading the simple life for studying in the city. One day, I would be Meadow Williams, editor and chief, and no one was stopping me.

What was not so simple, however, was Weston Ridge. My best friend from pre-k through high school turned insanely hot the summer between 8th grade and Freshman year, so I snatched him up before anyone else could. He came from a bloodline thick with generations of farmers and the looks of a J-Crew model. We were the "it" couple all through our high school career. It was a dream. He was a dream. The cliche was tall, dark, and handsome cowboy was actually his profile. A true farmboy, genetically designed to be a rancher. Athletic and rugged with a soft side that was endearing. He was a stud and not just sexy but sweet, funny, and genuinely kind, too. A heart of gold laid deep within his hunky physic. I was just 5'5, so he towered over me at 6'2. I loved looking up at him, gazing into his rich sapphire blue eyes. His golden skin and adoring dimples made him even more irresistible. I loved him. I think I had always loved him one way or another. His dreams were different than mine, though, and we both had known that. He was always destined to take over his family's business and become a local leader. It was in his DNA.

It was our last summer of love before we parted ways. He was staying close and attending the University of Kentucky while I had my eyes set somewhere much further for college. We agreed that a long-distance relationship wasn't anything that either of us wanted. We enjoyed the time we had together and every minute in between. Weston's family was a legacy in our town and he was proud to continue the tradition one day. He would follow in his father's footsteps as he did his father, and so on. His mother, however, was also a local entrepreneur herself. Weston was spawned into generational greatness. His mother, Meredith, was born and raised in that small town, cooked the best fried chicken, raised three boys, and was a banker. By 'banker,' I mean her family owned a chain of financial institutions, 36 to be exact.

They began in Versailles, Kentucky, and had expanded in the south and midwest over the past 80 years. She was now active president of the institution and had been for about 3 years now. She was in her early fifties, but you wouldn't guess she was over 40. Stunning and petite, prim and proper, with long black hair that shined like glass. Big boss lady who was so incredibly soft-spoken, well-mannered, and kind but could also throw down Buffalo Trace like it was iced tea. Her grace and hometown hospitality made her incredibly admirable. You would never know she was worth millions unless you visited her walk-in closet.

His Father, Richard Ridge, was a farmer whose family had been around since the beginning of the town itself. Shaping it, developing its beginning, creating jobs, and implementing the farm industry. They were the Rockefellers of Versailles, and they even had a street named after them, Ridge Lane. He also was a farm manager and had his best year ever, selling over 14 million. He was the definition of a silver fox. Baby blue eyes that literally twinkled when he grinned, and he had the whitest teeth of anyone I've ever seen. With his mom being a gorgeous, small-town socialite and his dad resembling Robert Redford circa 1990, my boyfriend Weston Ridge was the dream boat you would imagine. Both of their families had roots in our town, and he was the golden boy with the golden ticket.

He got his jet-black hair from his mom, along with her sharp eye structure and adorable dimples. Weston's shimmering blue eyes, broad shoulders, and swagger were all from his dad. He was a glorified country boy and proud of it. The true definition of a heartthrob. The dynamic of our relationship over time as childhood friends to dating and, eventually, lovers had been an adventure and truly incredible experience for a small-town girl like me. Literally, anything and everything you'd expect from a Hallmark movie. I couldn't be luckier, and he couldn't be sexier. Even though we were about to embark on new adventures and go our separate ways, the memories would never leave. Maybe fade but never leave.

I was sad to leave him and would miss him dearly, but our paths were different. The thought of leaving my parents, however, made my stomach turn. I had never been away from them my entire life, other than a sleepover at a friend's house or a weekend with Grandma. My mom and dad were the best. My best friends, best supporters, best protectors, best everything. They were the cutest couple, always were. I know all marriages are not ideal, and arguing and fighting are common and occur. Yet, I can only remember one time my parents ever fought to where voices were raised. One time in the 18 years they raised me. Either they really had it all figured out or were just really good at hiding it.

I can actually remember the fight as if it were yesterday. It was in 1989, and I was five years old. It was Christmas morning. My eyes had been set on one present in particular, a rectangle-shaped box that resembled the gift I wished for most of all. When my dad passed it over to me, my heart leaped with excitement. As I ripped open my present, doe-eyed and anxious as can be, my parents sat before me, staring in anticipation of my reaction. My mom had the Polaroid ready, and I'm pretty sure Dad already had poured some Jack into his coffee. Christmas morning magic laced with ribbons and bows, graced with smiles and laughter.

As I shredded the red and green reindeer wrapping paper, the gift was slowly becoming exposed. It couldn't be, it isn't?! Oh My God!! It is! The only gift I wanted that year was a Cabbage Patch doll. I was elated, jumping up and down, screaming, crying, and squeezing the doll until my knuckles had turned bright white. This was the best day ever. As I was consumed by my own joy and loud cheers, I hardly noticed the argument engulfing me in front of me.

My mother, enraged, stood up with her arms waving in the air and screaming at the top of her lungs. My dad hangs his head low with disappointment to avoid making any sort of eye contact with her. Evidently, my father was in charge of retrieving the doll during the holiday season. Although he waited in line for 2 hours, as my mom had ordered him to, he grabbed the 'wrong' doll. Apparently, mama's order was to pick up the blonde doll, so she matched me. Dad grabbed the girl with brown hair instead. It did not matter to me which one I had. I was just thrilled to even own one. She forgave Dad for his misfortune within just a couple of short hours. He caught her under the mistletoe, and it was over. Pretty high standards for a relationship where the only fight they had ever had was over buying me the 'wrong' doll. Oof. I still tease my dad about it to this day. I know my mom appreciates it by the size of her smile each time I bring it up. I was one lucky kid to have these two gems.

My mom and dad were also high school sweethearts, as most people were in the area. Larry and Jennifer Williams are high school sweethearts who are still madly in love. My mom was the definition of a blonde bombshell, even in her forties. She had just a few wrinkles that were lining the base of her dark, sultry eyes. The deep, chocolate-brown tone mirrored an earthy gaze. She was also small-framed and barely taller than me. Her blonde locks were typically thrown up in a messy bun with wispy strands falling to her face. Everyone adored her, especially my dad. He was always smitten around her, calling her his hometown hottie. She had been the county fair queen in 1977, after all.

My Dad stood tall and lean with sandy blond hair and beaming blue eyes. The kind that sparkled when he shared stories and lit up when my mom walked in the room. He was kind and approachable, fun and mischievous. He could make Mom laugh for hours, grill the best Ribeye around, and rope a steer like no one else. He was my hero. The weekends were my favorite. That's when we rode our horses until the sun would set, and Mom would call out for dinner. During the last couple of summers, I worked side by side with them at our family business. They owned a furniture store 7 miles up the road. My

Dad cut and crafted the pieces, and my Mom managed the business. They were a great team. They shared the same views and ideas, and everything was so incredibly seamless and streamlined for them. They had the perfect marriage, one I could only hope for one day.

I was an only child due to my mom having a couple of miscarriages before my birth. Because of that, they gave me the love they would have spread among a herd of kids. I was so blessed. You would have thought I was lonely because I did not have any siblings, but it was quite the opposite. My parents and I were so close that there was never any feeling of void within our family. I would miss them while I was away at school but I knew they had each other and would be just fine.

It has been one month since our high school graduation. We sat in the back of that F-150 once again. It was two-toned, pearl white with a navy stripe along the side panels. Lift kit made it stand tall, and the engine roared when he fired it up. My favorite sound in the world was hearing it coming down my parents driveway on that gravel rock. It meant he was almost to me. Weston kept an old wooden step stool in the back so I could hop on the tailgate easier since I'm so short. He was always so thoughtful and considerate. Always looking out for me, always making me smile and laugh. Perfect. Heaven right here on earth, in this little pasture in the middle of nowhere. It would be our last night under those shining stars, watching the deer slowly roam in the distance. Last night, he would brush my hair out of my face and lean in to kiss me under the glow of the moonlight. Last time, I would gaze at the shadow of his face and listen to his sweet, soft whispers in the dark. Last time, he would say he loved me with the shimmering pond reflecting in his eyes. Last night, before I left my roots to branch out for more.

I was headed up north to the big city, Chicago. I had always dreamed of what was out there beyond this rural retreat I called home. Buildings so tall they hide in the clouds, a tundra of iconic nightclubs, gourmet restaurants on every corner, luxury boutiques on Michigan Avenue, and overpriced, boujee loft apartments. What more could a girl ask for? I couldn't wait. I was beyond excited. Weston was perfect, but we were only 18. He needed someone planted in the plains, a housewife to come home to after spending hours in the fields. That's not what I wanted, at least not now. This was my time.

That next morning, I loaded up my silver 2000 Chevy Cavalier and headed off to Chi-town like a free bird. I had been accepted to the Chicago Arts Institute and was moving into my new apartment. Although school wouldn't start for a month and a half, I wanted to familiarize myself with the area. My mom and dad were leaving just a couple of hours after me to bring a small U-Haul with my bed and dresser. There was a local retailer picking up some pieces from my parents' shop, so they had to leave later in the day.

The long drive alone was both refreshing and reflecting. I was so proud of myself for taking a step to see the world. A dream I've always had was finally coming to life. I was nervous and excited. Butterflies were going crazy in my stomach as I got closer to the city. My heart did hurt thinking of leaving Weston, but our paths were always different. His future was the small town living and always will be. He will farm for his father and continue the Ridge legacy as he should.

He understood and supported my goals, celebrated my decision, and said he will love me always. He will always have a piece of my heart, but my head was simply in the clouds right now. I smiled as I drove into the sunset, thinking of that handsome boy. As I cruised and grinned, the peaks of towers started to show before me. There it was, the outline of the city ahead of me. I have arrived.

The sun was setting, and beams of light shone through the breaks in the buildings. The sprawling concrete towers set the scene for the lively city. I navigated through the busy streets to my new apartment located on campus. Although I had already been here before for a tour with my parents, I was still mesmerized. Architectural marvels everywhere, stunning and vast, just as the energy that filled the air. The earthy aroma from the Chicago River sprawled across the pavement. Colorful carts grazed the streets, offering delicacies from Italian beef to hotdogs smothered in grilled onions. Hundreds of people stroll the sidewalks, heading in every direction. You didn't see flannel shirts and cut-off jean shorts, but you did see savvy dresses and stilettos. Lavish Mercedes Benz and stylish Porches blew past me, taxis flying in and out of lanes, guys in Armani suits on scooters sliding through the streets. It was a whole new world with colorful people and beautiful buildings.

I pulled into the parking garage for my building and unloaded a couple of bags I had brought with me and a laundry basket full of snacks my Mom had packed. The scent of the city was arousing. The sound of the traffic and the presence of people everywhere was everything I desired. I loaded my belongings onto the elevator and headed down to the lobby. The building was absolutely beautiful, just as I remembered. So chic and modern, open and full of art, almost like a mini museum. The marble countertops were trimmed with LED lights that illuminated the front desk. A large chandelier hung above, ironically enough reminding me of the giant willow tree in my parents' front yard. The dazzling lights draped down above me just as the long, flowing tree branches had.

I approached a very tall and lean blonde at the front desk to sign in. Her eyes were warm, and her smile was welcoming as she motioned for me to come forward.

"Hello! Welcome, what is your name, dear? I will get your keys and a cart for your things."

Grinning from ear to ear with uncontrollable excitement, anxiety, and hope, I simply replied, "Thank you. I am Meadow Williams."

I have arrived.

# CHAPTER 2

*6 Years Later*

It's amazing the satisfaction you can find in the little things. As I placed my final set of silverware on the table, I stared in awe at the lovely arrangement I had spent the last 2 hours putting together. We were hosting a dinner party this evening, and I wanted it to be absolutely perfect. I had bought a new burgundy tablecloth that was so vibrant and lovely that it lit up the dining room, which was otherwise draped in beige, boring beige. The ebony porcelain dinner plates I special ordered from Neiman Marcus were stunning against the colorful linen and paired so elegantly with the black stemmed wine glasses.

I had three white orchids delivered earlier that day to place on the dining table. The color contrast was eye-catching and beautiful. Simple but stunning, everything I was going for. I had dimmed the lights so the room had a radiant glow that was intimate and inviting. The bar was complete with various wines, bourbons, gins, and cocktail condiments for old fashions and martins. I wasn't sure if I was more proud of my setup or just got pure joy from hosting.

I loved pleasing people and hosting gatherings. I think it was something I got from my upbringing. Sunday dinners at Grandma's were something I looked forward to every week. It wasn't just the food or just the people. It was all of it. I loved all of it. Hosting my own dinner parties as an adult gave me that feeling again every time, something to look forward to. As I roamed the room, panning for any imperfections, I grinned to myself. Pleased with the perfection that was set before me. My husband would be home soon, and I wanted to be sure every detail was complete and that the room was picturesque.

Ryan Cooper is a hotel entrepreneur, investor, CEO, and my husband. We met in my second year of college and married two months after I graduated. Ryan was five years older than me and very established in Chicago. We met when I began working at the Four Seasons as a front desk agent my sophomore year. He was conducting a meeting in one of the property's boardrooms, and we literally ran into each other in the hallway. It was love at first sight. Ryan had hazelnut brown hair and eyes so steel and dark that it was hard to distinguish the iris from the pupil. He was gorgeous, intense, and smart. A natural leader, a young elite, who was determined and driven. He had a million-dollar smile to go along with his bank account and was sharp and sexy in his $3,000 suits. I imagine that a wealthy and intelligent socialite with family ties throughout the city would be part of the reason for his great success. I had never met someone so young and aggressive. If there was something he wanted, nothing would stop him from getting it. He invested young with some inheritance money he received from his great-grandfather. Ryan had some friends on Wall Street who, very graciously and probably somewhat illegally, guided him to make successful choices with his ventures across the country as well.

A suited millionaire before 30 years old and he fell in love with a little country girl from the sticks. Never in my wildest dreams would I have expected this lavish life. Far from the backwoods and country roads, I now sat high, scraping the sky and towering over the city streets in this extravagant home on the Gold Coast. Luxurious and lakefront, the turquoise water was hugging the affluent neighborhood. The ritzy and righteous consumed the real estate within the treasured rich community. Lush trees lined the streets before the beautiful stately homes and historic churches. We lived in a sprawling 7,000-square-foot condo that sat atop one of the most coveted streets, offering breathtaking views of the city and lake. It was captivating and timeless, from the marvel staircase to curved custom cabinetry. 6 bedrooms and three charming terraces that infused an abundance of light from the sun's rays. It was extravagant and grand, boosting an elegant tone as fireplaces illuminated every room, spreading grace and warmth throughout the mansion. This is the life I sought, the life I always wanted, or at least I thought I did.

As I peered up at the clock, I realized Ryan would be home any minute from work. The subtle light shining in would soon fade along with my smile. Everything has a price. The glitz and glamor that captivated and impressed me are the very things that now harness my soul. Ryan's aggressive nature, which was once appealing and sexy, was now smothering and suppressing. I felt like Rapunzel, trapped in the castle where no one could hear me. No one can save me. His passionate presence was no longer endearing. It was deceiving and dangerous. His control and rage exploded on me once the ink hit the paper. His violent temper erupted daily, no longer sweeping me off my feet but knocking me off them.

"How's my baby girl today?" Ryan walked into the room, extending his hands out to me.

I approached him with open arms and slid into him, embracing his hug. He leaned out just enough to kiss me or begin to kiss me. He pushed me slowly aside, staring past my lips, which he was just locked on. I turned my body around to see what he was glaring at so intently.

"Oh baby, do you love my dining setup? I worked so hard on it today."

"No, Meadow, I don't."

My smile shifted abruptly, and I could feel my heart begin to race. He was mad. I hate it when he is mad. Clearing my throat before replying to him, trying to control the quiver in my tone before I spoke.

"I'm so sorry honey, what is it that you don't like? I have plenty of time to fix whatever it is," I said optimistically to him, trying not to show my fear.

He slowly walked around the table, peering down as his fingertips softly ran along the fabric. He then suddenly paused, and his hand stood still on the table. He stared intensely, almost as if in a trance, down at the table. Silent, still, transfixed. What was he looking at? I didn't understand what was wrong and was not about to ask. Unfortunately, I knew he was about to tell me exactly what he didn't like.

"Well, Meadow, I guess I personally don't understand why you would go through all of this effort to set a table over a linen full of wrinkles. Have you looked around this place? Do we appear to be trash? Are you intentionally being careless to prove some kind of point about perfection? Are you blind or dumb, or perhaps both?"

"I have another tablecloth. I will just switch them out. I am so sorry. I suppose the excitement of hosting dinner caused me to be distracted and not notice. I will take care of it right now!"

I walked over swiftly to begin to clear the table to change the linen. I could feel him peering at me across the table, but I just looked down and began moving the candles from the table to the wet bar. I could see his body moving towards me as I scrambled to correct my mistake.

I had disappointed him. He does not tolerate disappointment. Ryan moved in even closer to me as I reached next for the salt and pepper shakers. Then, the monster came out. He lunged at me, grabbing my right arm and spinning me around. Now clutching both of my arms with his immense grip, shoving me backward until my back smacked against the wall. Jolting my body, pulling me back to him, and then thrusting me into the wall again, over and over. Slamming my body so hard and with such intense force I thought I was going to go through the drywall.

"Look at what you've done, Meadow. Your pure laziness and inconsideration have now gotten me upset. Do you think I enjoy doing this? It's almost like you provoke me at times."

He held my arms tight to keep me in place and grabbed my chin with his free hand, forcing me to look towards the table.

"Do you purposely try to sabotage everything, Meadow? Do you find it amusing to embarrass me with these little stunts you pull? How could you possibly not notice the wrinkles? I think you did it on purpose," still squeezing my chin so hard with his thumb and index finger, holding my face firm.

"No! Why would you say something like that? I would never want to embarrass you. I wanted this to be flawless and perfect, just for you, dear. I swear, I would never..."

Before I could spit another word out, he released the grasp he had on my chin, drew back his arm, and smacked me across the face. This wasn't one of his usual slaps. This one was with the back of his hand. When I got one of these, he was really pissed off. These ones always hurt the worst. In fact, this one dropped me right to my knees.

"YOU DUMB BITCH!" He screamed as he kicked me in my side so hard that he lifted my petite 5'5" frame right off the ground.

"Please stop, PLEASE! I will fix it. Just let me go so I can fix it all. Please stop."

I pleaded for mercy, but it was too late. When he started, it was like unleashing a lion. He grabbed me by the back of the hair and pulled me off the ground. He guided me to the table, where he pushed my face into the same fabric that I had just admired moments ago. My face smacked the top of the table as he held it down with one hand. Jarring the remaining dishes left on the inadequate table.

"I'm going to go shower now, Meadow. When I come back this all better be fixed."

He let go of me and walked towards the doorway. I slowly raised up, adjusting my hair and wiping the mascara that was running down my flushed cheeks. He stopped abruptly on his way out of the room and turned back towards me.

"Actually, I don't like these fucking glasses either. Get rid of them too." He then grabbed the glass closest to him and chucked it at the wall, shattering it into a thousand little iridescent pieces all over the floor. "Clean that shit up, too, while you're at it."

He finally left the room, and I stood there still, in awe at the table before me. Different from before now. Not with pride from a sense of accomplishment but now in disgust and detriment. I had a little more than an hour before our guests were to arrive to clean up the mess of the dining room and the mess that was now my face.

I walked into the kitchen to grab the broom and dustpan from the pantry closet. As I moved through the hallway, I passed the vintage, 20th-century mirror that hung in the center wall between the two rooms. I loved this mirror. I found it on eBay for $150 dollars when I moved to the city, which was the first thing I purchased for my apartment. Walking past it every day was something I unconsciously enjoyed more than I realized. It wasn't just because of the sheer beauty of this mirror that felt more like a piece of artwork with its bold, textured frame stretching 3x5 ft across the wall. It was actually because of what it symbolized, my FIRST purchase for MY first apartment in THE city. A reminder of where I started and the hopes and dreams I unpacked the first day I came to town. Endless opportunities, aspirations, and dreams coming true were now overshadowed by shattered glass and broken ribs.

As I walked past the mirror, I caught a piece of my reflection in my peripheral vision. I stopped abruptly, stunned and shaken. Who was this girl? My hair was tattered and tangled, cheeks red and puffy, so swollen it looked as if I'd just had dental surgery. Eyes bloodshot and watering abundantly. My makeup was smeared and smudged, and my eyes were already turning greenish/brown from where he smacked me.

I had everything I ever wanted. Was this the price I had to pay to have it, though? The simple farm life suddenly didn't sound so bad, but it was far gone, and so was I. Meadow Cooper was here now. I wiped my tears and brushed back my hair, put my head up, continued towards the closet, and grabbed the broom. People were arriving soon. I needed to pull myself together.

'Ding, Ding.' The doorbell rang, thankfully breaking through the silence and tension running through the house. Our guests had arrived.

"Hello my beautiful friend!" Celeste shouted as she held up a bottle of Dom Pereon and strutted through the front door.

Celeste Taylor and I had become best friends working at the hotel during college. She was actually married to one of Ryan's hotel investors, so we frequently double-dated. She was the best. So beautiful and poised but with the mouth of a sailor. Celeste and I looked like complete opposites but got along like sisters. Her long, blonde hair shined like glass under the entry lights of our home. Tall and thin, with high cheekbones and a killer fashion sense. She was essentially a live, walking Barbie. Eloquent and charming but savvy and sharp.

Polar opposite of me, I wish I could be bold and confident like her. Celeste's husband, Tom, was a different breed than Ryan. In fact, they were so different. I don't believe they were so much friends as partners who had to dedicate a certain amount of time and trust to each other. Tom was laid back and hilarious, not stern and serious like Ryan. I almost felt at times that Tom simply tolerated Ryan because of their work situation, and I honestly could never blame him for that.

"The place looks amazing and it smells so good in here!" Celeste sat the bottle of champagne down to grab me with both arms and squeeze me so tight.

She was a hugger, and even more so when she drank. It used to annoy me when we first met, but now I look forward to it. I suppose after being hit more than hugged the last few years, I've learned to appreciate the sweet embrace.

"I'm going to get the charcuterie board and will bring it to the living room, guys. Why don't you guys grab a cocktail and we will be right there. Come on, Celeste, be my assistant, please."

I grabbed the bottle of champagne and walked with Celeste into the kitchen.

"Hmmmm, look at this spread girl!" Celeste walked around the kitchen island, admiring the charcuterie station. She may have supermodel vibes, but her appetite did not reflect that. "How long did it take you to put this thing together?"

"Not as long as it did at the dinner table," I replied snarly.

"What is special about the dining table," Celeste asked, leaning back and looking through the doorway to the dining room.

Peeking her head back in towards me, confused.

"I don't get it," she said. "I mean, it's cute and all, love the flowers. Did you fold the napkins fancy or some shit?"

I laughed and shook my head. Another reason we were such good friends. She can always make me laugh, and not even intentionally, which I appreciated even more.

"Nothing, I was just kidding," I put my head down and walked over to the other side of the island to grab the board.

She grabbed my hand mid-reach.

"Stop it. Look at me now, Meadow."

I couldn't look up right away; my eyes began to tear up, and I knew if I looked up into hers, the flooding would come. I was at a breaking point, and she was the one who could break me.

"I'm fine, Celeste. Let's talk about it later," I said as I motioned my head to the living room in which Tom and Ryan sat.

Her face instantly changed. Her doe-eyed, warm-hearted eyes shifted downwards. Her eyebrows now frowned, and her nostrils flared. Those perfectly penciled lips pressed firmly together and perched. She squeezed my hand and leaned closer to me.

"Not again, Meadow. Did he hit you again?"

"I said let's talk about it later. Not the right place or time, if he hears us...if he hears us, well, it will just make it worse. Shhh, later, please."

She sighed and looked at me with such sadness that it made my heart hurt. She was my best friend, really my only friend in Chicago, and at this point, I wasn't sure how much of our friendship was just sympathy for me. She was so good to me but I just hated the pity I saw in her eyes. Her genuine concern was so comforting at times but also distracting and overwhelming at other times. I couldn't leave him, and because of that, I think she thought less of me. I'm sure it's in my head, but the looks, the hopeless looks she gave were more than I could bear at times. I never wanted her to know how bad it was, and I tried to hide it from her for a long time. Gradually, she would notice different marks, actions, or behaviors in which she picked up on what was happening.

She let go of my hand and took a small step back from me. Giving up on the battle for the moment and hearing my request. She nods her head slowly and forces a smile onto her face. Reaching up slowly with her left hand, she brushes back the hair falling over my battered eye.

She softly whispers, "You just don't deserve this, Meadow. It has to stop."

Looking into her eyes, trying not to break, I take a deep breath and look right back at her, holding my tears in with every bit of strength I have.

"It's just a bruise."

# CHAPTER 3

It's just a bruise. It's just a mark. It's just a fracture. It's just another incident, another excuse, another time. It wasn't always like this, though. It started out as lust and turned to lashes. From the day we met, he swept me off my feet. I felt like I was on top of the world during that time, happier than I'd ever been. I had everything I had ever wanted and dreamed of.

Those first couple of years in Chicago were everything I had hoped it would be. School was amazing, my job was great, I loved everything the busy city life offered, and to top it off, I was dating Chicago's most eligible bachelor. Life couldn't be any better. He was such an impressive man. Young, sexy, smart, and incredibly poised. So much more mature and sophisticated than other guys his age. Although he was very intense and conservative when it came to business matters, when we were alone, he was the complete opposite. He was fun and loving, even playful at times. He was literally the man of my dreams, or any woman's for that matter.

How did a little small-town girl land the sexiest man in the windy city with a bank account that could buy the very city? My weekends went from float trips to helicopter rides that hovered below the heavens and over the sparkle of the city. I was 21 at this time and living an absolute fairy tale. Far from the farm now, I had found my prince charming. Life was no longer simple and boring but perfect and magical. At least, I thought it was. I should have known right then that it wasn't real because fairy tales don't exist.

The first time he hit me was on our honeymoon. Four days in

Montego Bay, staying at the Iberostar resort had been absolute bliss. Panoramic views of the clear, emerald-blue sea laid before me. Captivating for miles and miles until you could no longer see where the sky ended and the ocean began. The sand was soft as silk as my feet slid through it, gliding almost as if on ice. The resort was lush and luxurious, with exotic foods and exquisite cocktails. Supreme staffing and state-of-the-art architecture. The landscaping was colorful and creative, so green and lush. Everywhere you turned, it was so grand and impressive, breathtaking, really. I had never seen anything like this. It was truly the definition of paradise. It was picturesque, and I was in love. I never wanted this to end.

We would get up early every morning, eat out on the balcony, and then head out to the beach before it got too busy. It was a private beach, exclusive to the hotel, but the peace it delivers when no one else is around is unmatchable. Then, we would pick an adventure to mark off our honeymoon bucket list. First day, we snorkeled in the enchanting sea next to fluorescent fish and brilliantly bright coral. Then, we embarked on a sailboat shipping champagne and spotting dolphins. The 3rd day, we sliced through the Caribbean Sea on matching jet skis. Riding the waves in the sea salt breeze was so invigorating, freeing, and fun. The water shimmered under the blazing sun as I raced my handsome husband back to the golden sandy shore. I was having the time of my life.

The fourth morning, we decided to take a break from extracurricular activities and just enjoy some R&R by the pool. The pool was just as impressive as the rest of the property, as expected. Lavish and large, just steps from the sand and is engulfed with palm trees and beach chairs. Swim-up bars and butlers with snack services. Surrounded by tropical gardens and just feet away from gourmet restaurants, yet you could still hear the crashing of the ocean waves. It was serene and surreal. Poolside was a day of fun on its own. The spectacular views and amenities, this was refreshing.

"Cheers, baby," Ryan held up his frozen lime margarita towards me. "To new beginnings, my wife, now and forever."

I grabbed my cocktail eagerly to match his, "Cheers, my love! Thank you for making me the happiest girl on earth. I will be yours forever."

He took a sip of his drink and sat his glass on the lip of the pool next to us. He turned towards me with the biggest, sexiest grin. He had a million-dollar smile, just like Tom Cruise. He could light up a room, and I loved every bit of it. He bent his knees as he came towards me, lowering his body into the pool of water. Going further down and deeper as he approached until he was all the way under water, and under me.

"REVERSE CANNON BALL!" he shouted once he had thrust himself out of the water while launching me into the air.

I crashed into the water, trying to contain my laughter so I didn't choke while underwater. I popped out to find him waiting for me with a towel above the pool. Looking down at me, the sun cascading off his back, tiny droplets of water trickle out from his hair. The shadow cast over his eyes, but the gleam of his sexy smile I could see clearly.

"Come on, Meadow babe, let's go grab another drink."

We headed over to the tiki bar which really resembles more of a pavilion with dried grass draped all over it. This was no ordinary tiki, grand and gorgeous as every other amenity the facility had to offer. Situated between the seductive pool and shimmering sea, I wasn't sure which direction to look. I ordered another Bahama Mama, which I had become a fan of the day before, and asked for the food menu. The sun sure did bring out my appetite. I was starving. As I was surfing the menu, Ryan's phone rang.

As he grabbed it to answer, he looked towards me and pointed to the menu, "Order me some shrimp cocktail, dear. I'm going to take this call, and I'll be right back. It's work, won't be long."

He kissed me on the forehead and walked away towards the hotel.

The bartender took my order just moments after, and then I sat back in my chair and looked over my shoulder, staring off into the sparkling shores. Drifting away and dazed, I heard a voice behind me that startled me in my tranquil state.

"Excuse me, ma'am, are you done with that menu?"

A younger man, probably around my age, was standing next to me along the bar, leaning on the slate countertop, "Ma'am?"

"Oh, I'm so sorry!" I bashfully replied. "You caught me in a trance. Yes, here, I am finished, and it's all yours." I slid him the menu across the bar.

"Thank you," he kindly replied. "Didn't mean to disturb you," he joked. "Any recommendations?"

"It's actually our first time trying food from this bar. I'd imagine it's great since everything else we've had has been amazing." I replied. "We're here on our honeymoon, just day 4 so still in a sample mood of what the hotel has to offer."

"Same here! We just got here last night, but my bride Sarah is right over there," he grinned and proudly pointed across the garden to the pool, where a lovely blond in a crochet white cover-up waved back and blew a kiss.

"Awww, that's awesome. Well, congrats to you both. Nice meeting you, have fun!" I raised my glass to him and towards his wife in the distance.

He nodded and said, "Same to you!" as he walked off towards Sarah with the menu in hand.

"Who was that Meadow?"

Ryan had snuck up behind me, scaring me right out of my bar stool. I giggled and turned back towards him, throwing my arms around him, "Baby!! You scared me! Is everything ok with work, dear?"

He pulled my arms down from the sides of his neck and sat them in my lap very firmly. Very firmly, held them there with so much pressure it began to hurt.

"Ryan, what's wrong?"

He stared at me with his defined dark eyes, cold and focused. No more million-dollar smile. His lips were tight, clenched. His temple throbbing, and his hands squeezing mine tightly. He had never looked at me this way before, so intense, so angry. Was he being serious?

"Ryan, what is the matter with you?" I whispered, as I didn't want to draw any attention to other resort guests or the bartender.

"Who in the fuck was that Meadow? Simple question, who the fuck was that you were speaking to while I was gone?"

"Oh! That was just some guy grabbing a menu. Yeah, super nice just got here with his new bride last night. Just on his honeymoon, like us! Was that what you were mad about? I'm so sorry. He was just up here for a minute. It was completely harmless."

"Harmless? Do you think embarrassing me or tarnishing my reputation is harmless, Meadow? For a man just requesting a menu, you sure seem to find plenty to talk about besides what to order."

"Please don't think that, Ryan. I swear there was nothing to it. I would never do that. HE is here with his wife like I'm here with my husband, just needed a menu, babe. I'm sorry, let's drop it. We're having so much fun. Let's not let a little misunderstanding ruin our time."

"Lunch is served, Mr. and Mrs. Cooper."

The bartender arrived with our order and placed our plates before us.

Before our dishes even hit the bar top, Ryan intervened, "Actually, we will be taking these to go. Could you round us up a couple of boxes, please, and put the bill on our room tab?"

"Why can't we eat here, Ryan? I'm absolutely famished."

"Box up the fucking food Meadow. We are going back to the room now."

I said no more, boxed up the food, and followed behind him like a scolded child, lingering behind their parents once they realized they were in trouble. Looking down at my feet the entire way, nervous and anxious. I had never seen him act like this before. I didn't know what to say or do. I walked cautiously behind him into the resort and down the hallway to the elevator doors.

I continued to look down at the to-go boxes in my hand, avoiding eye contact and hoping the fuse in his temper would burn out before we cleared the penthouse floor. The doors opened, and he walked in first. I followed behind and took a stance next to him in the elevator. A couple of people walked by, but no one got in the elevator. As the doors began to slowly shut in front of me, I then really wished those people needed the elevator.

He glanced over at me as I stood stiff and silent in the elevator. He started to produce a slight grin and tilted his head towards mine. *Is he better now?* He doesn't seem as hostile and angry now, good, we can continue to enjoy our honeymoon.

"Meadow honey," he said, looking into my eyes.

"Yes, dear," I replied with a small smile, seeing if he was warming back up to finally.

"As my wife, I assumed you would naturally know to support me, agree with me, essentially be aware that you are always a representation of me. Therefore, when I tell you to do or not to do something, you do it. No questions, no arguing, just fucking do it."

I was so confused. What had I done? "Ryan, I'm sorry, but I don't know what I did that was going against you. What are you talking about?"

His sly grin turned sinister in a split second. He stood up straight, off of the wall, and took a step towards me. With one swift swing, he smacked the boxes right out of my hand. Crushed styrofoam, jumbo shrimp, and shreds of my salmon Caesar salad exploded in the compacted space. His hands grabbed my neck with such speed and force that I was completely blindsided. I felt helpless, weak, shocked, and scared. He squeezed my neck so tight I was immediately breathless and panicked. Pushing me back against the steel wall, slamming my body so easily as if I were just a rag dog. His eyes were black as coal and fierce. Looking into them, he seemed so empty and evil. It was bizarre and frightening. How could someone be so loving and fun and suddenly snap? I couldn't breathe. I tried to kick my legs, but he pressed his body so tight and close against mine I couldn't move. My fingers dug into his clenching hands, desperately trying to pry them off to breathe.

"You are mine, Meadow, all fucking mine. Signed, sealed, and delivered as of four days ago. You will not disrespect me by entertaining another man. You will not embarrass me by being flattered by another man. I give you an exquisite life, and you will not take it for granted and act like a spoiled bitch. Remember, I gave you this life you wanted so badly, and I can just as easily take it away. Do you understand how to behave now? Is this going to be an issue, Meadow?"

I shook my left and right aggressively, tears streaming down my face. Trying to mumble, "no," but couldn't barely squeeze out a peep.

He slowly released his tight grip around my throat. He backed up gradually and finally, fully let go of me. He brushed the hair out of my eyes and wiped my tears.

"Good wife."

The elevator pinged, and the door opened, "We're here, Meadow. Hurry and clean that mess up, then come to the room."

He stepped out of the elevator and strutted towards our suite with the room key and beach towel in hand. It felt like an eternity waiting for the elevator doors to shut with me now alone inside. As they finally came to a complete close, I dropped to my knees on the exquisite marble floor below me and began to pick up what was once our lunch and now the debris of our first fight. Looking around me, beside myself, I began to cry. *Did I marry a monster?*

# CHAPTER 4

After the honeymoon, things were never the same. I felt as if I was now living with a stranger. He was possessive, controlling, and condescending. It was as if once the marriage papers were signed, I became ownership. Another piece of property for him to play with and show off. Except, there wasn't much play, more punishment. He had standards and expectations that were never to fall lower than perfection. He was a control freak in every aspect of his life, and I had become his new object to obsess over.

I had restrictions and rules. I wasn't allowed to work, not even discuss it. The utter idea was absurd to him, and he actually found it to be disrespectful. I wouldn't recognize myself if you showed me 6 years ago who I became. My passion and dreams turned to orders and fear.

"What woman would want to work when she has a life like this? You are so ungrateful. It's sickening Meadow. Do you know how many women would trade to be in your expensive ass Louboutin shoes that you so proudly strut around in? As if you could afford those if you weren't with me, you fucking hillbilly," he once said. I know, quite the charmer.

Dinner had to be ready every day promptly at 6:30 pm and up to par. Full course meal, table set for a king, and I better not dare ever burn anything. I learned that the hard way once. It took weeks for the blisters to heal on my hands after he threw a pan of bubbling hot lasagna at me. The edges were apparently too "crispy" for his liking. Along with dinner, the house was to always be tidy and clean. I also did a run-through before he came home each evening. I would make sure all the artwork and photos on the walls were perfectly straight. Never ever let there be a crooked frame in sight. Throw pillows were also to be placed in the corners of the couches at a 45-degree angle. The sherpa blanket that laid across the back of the couch, had to be folded evenly from corner to corner and could not hang without being absolutely symmetrical. I made sure to always hang his clothes in the closet based on coordination of color and style. I dusted daily and washed the floors on my hands and knees. It was easier to eliminate any possible streaking that a mop might leave behind this way.

I couldn't leave the house without telling him first where I was going, when, and with who. He claimed he was always just concerned about my safety, but I know that wasn't the truth. His pride was his top concern. He simply wanted to always have tabs on me and not let me get too far. His jealousy was insane and out of control. I had anxiety anytime we were to attend an event or even so much as go out for dinner. I learned over time to avoid looking in the direction of any man, ever. When in conversation with one, such as a waiter taking my order, I would never make eye contact with them. The most simple gesture could be misunderstood by Ryan as a threat, flirtation, sign of disrespect, or, worst of all, competition. I made certain to never give any man any equal or greater attention than to him. It had made me introverted and disinterested in any social activities at this point. I wanted to stay locked in my room, hidden from the world. My ambition and excitement that I brought with me to the city had now turned to misery and fear.

My father passed away the year after we were married from a heart attack. Gone in a matter of minutes with no warning, no symptoms, no goodbye. I wasn't allowed to attend his funeral. Ryan had some business matters in London to handle and, therefore, did not want me to go alone. I went anyway. When I returned to Chicago, I was in the hospital for 3 weeks after that beating. The amount of bruising, internal bleeding, and fractures raised enough suspicion for the hospital staff to contact the police. I lied to them and said the elevator at our penthouse was under repair and fell like a clutz running down the stairs. Silly me.

"I'm really sorry, Meadow. But, if you just wouldn't defy me, this wouldn't happen. Please stop making me do this to you; I don't enjoy it one bit." He reached out and gracefully touched my hand, softly stroking the top of it with his fingertips, back and forth. He leaned down and kissed the top of my hand, in which my IV was sticking out.

Not long after my father passed away, my mother had a stroke. I chose not to tell Ryan she survived. I wanted to return to be with her one day and couldn't let him know. He would never imagine me returning to my roots, as in his head, there was nothing there to go back to. I wanted it to remain that way. I called her exactly at 9 am every morning. I knew Ryan had a mandatory staff meeting at that time each day, so for 45 minutes, I was unmonitored. The stroke had sent her into dementia. Her memory wasn't stable. I wanted her to recognize my voice and know me. I was worried about slipping from her memory altogether.

I set her up with a lovely assisted living facility in Lexington that kept her social and busy, key things to help stimulate someone's brain who is going through dementia. I paid the bill monthly with a credit card I'd had since college that Ryan didn't know about. This way, it would never be traceable to any of our bank accounts for him to see. My dad paid the bill all the way until he passed. I think he loved the thought of me always having my own little nest egg provided by him. Before the stroke, my mom set it on auto pay and wanted to keep doing it in his honor. What did I say, my parents are/were the best.

I yearned to be with my mom. It was breaking my heart not to be with her right now. I missed my dad so much and felt tremendous guilt since his passing for not making more time these last few years to see him, see them. This was a rude and hurtful wakeup call, life truly is so short and so fragile. I know all my dad ever wanted was the best for me. But my searching out there for the best thing caused me to leave behind better things. I just didn't know. No one knew then or now what would happen. I never told a soul about the abuse. Celeste was my best friend, and after seeing various marks and bruises on me, I had confided in her. I couldn't tell anyone else. I was humiliated, ashamed, scared mostly. He threatened to kill me if I ever went to the police, said he'd find me if I ever left, and that no one could ever have me if he couldn't. I was trapped in a toxic manager with a very twisted, rich, and powerful man. Not exactly the adjectives you look for in a Tinder profile.

I have wanted to run away for so long now. I wanted to run so fast, all the way home. Reflecting on this whirlwind of a life that I have lived over the last few years was unsettling. My aspirations of becoming a fashion editor fell flat, my millionaire man with a million-dollar smile was actually an abusive narcissist, and the city lights were no longer enchanting for me. In fact, when I gazed off my terrace to the outstretched city, the shadows on the streets are what I now noticed more. The darkness that lurked below me. My visionary perspective of the city was once consumed by shimmer and shine but now was dim and dreadful. The light wasn't as bright anymore, the unilluminated areas seemed to consume my line of site.  It reminded me of the change in Ryan. Once bright, warm, and full of hope. Now cold, dark, and dangerous.

*I will leave one day.* I tell myself that every day. Every. Single. *Day. I will leave one of these days. Walk right out the door. Trade my Betty Johnsons for boots and Tesla for a tent. I have never missed home more. I missed it so much.* He would find me, though; I knew he would. Although he never took any interest in my background, family, or even where I came from, I knew he would still find me. Money and power go much further than ignorance. Unfortunately, I had to have a plan before I could ever leave, or I just kill myself now. The simplicity of the country was the new dream. It had always been a dream. I was just always blinded by the lights. I needed the dream but had to leave this lurking nightmare first.

Ryan was a person of routine, so I followed suit. I took advantage of knowing his calendar to plan my escape. Besides hiding my mother, I had also begun taking money from our bank accounts over the last several months. I take small amounts that, if ever questioned, could be justified as a "fundraiser donation" or something of that nature. I had a small bag packed and hidden inside a container marked, 'gardening tools.' Since he isn't much on getting his hands dirty, I figured he'd never find it. *One day, the timing will be right for me to grab it and go.*

When in an abusive relationship, the question always asked is, "Why didn't you just leave." Fear. Fear is ultimately the number one reason why. If you don't understand this, then consider yourself lucky. They tell you they will find you. They say you will always be theirs. They say they will kill you. Crazy and controlling, combined with money and power, make it even more challenging to leave. Not only leave but not be found. I was scared to run but more scared to stay. I couldn't call the police. It would just piss him off more. Anyone in Chicago knew Ryan one way or another. I was the young, hot entrepreneur, and I was the noble trophy wife. No one could ever know our secret. How dare we displace our perfect image. There was no crisis center I could trust, no social worker I could confide in, and no friend who could take me in. Celeste was my only friend and her husband was a friend and business partner to Ryan. No protection or direction was available to me. I was the only one who could save myself.

I grew up in Versailles, known for rodeos, distilleries, and our very own castle. Beautiful town full of farmers, cowboys, and the American dream. When I first met Ryan, I felt so intimidated by his status that I told him I was from Lexington. It's a larger city that houses a ton of manufacturing companies and leading brand industries. I thought it made me sound more appealing and established in a sense, not such a country bumpkin. I never felt good enough for him, even from the beginning. I guess that was my sign that it wasn't right, but it is hard to always read clearly with blurred lines.

The benefit of his narcissism was that everything was about him. Therefore, he never really questioned my past. Never saw a photo album from my childhood, scrolled through an old yearbook of mine, and once visited my parents back home. We married in Chicago, which is essentially the only life he knew of mine. In 6 years, the only time I returned home was to bury my father. If I could only get back home now, he would never find me. He would only search where he knew to look. He would never know about Versailles. Home is the key.

I made sure any mail pertaining to my mother's facility went to our home address in Kentucky, which I had forwarded to a PO box. Our neighbor kept the yard maintained and I had sold the horses a couple of years back. I couldn't wait for the day when I could pull back up that gravel driveway with my mom in the passenger seat. I desired a sunset from the front porch. Sweet tea and southern hospitality that I missed so much. Most of all, safety. I needed that comfort and to, ultimately, hold my mom's hand. Funny how things change. Life and style don't hold a candle to love and freedom. I had it all before I went searching for more.

I continued to daydream of horses and fields as I dusted the bookcase. I needed to finish cleaning soon so I could get ready for Ryan's work party. It was the 10-year anniversary of his brokerage firm, and we were to be at the Waldorf Astoria at 6 pm for cocktails before dinner. Another night of playing the role of the privileged and happy entrepreneur's wife. My conversations were to be kept minimal, I was never to be more witty than him at any moment, and

I had also learned to avoid eye contact with other men. My rules of engagement I suppose to not anger the beast. He was also very finicky over the outfits I wore to these events. I was to look classy and lovely but not sexy. Never upstage him but rather compliment him. I had to be sure there wasn't a scuff on my shoes or a loose thread on my dress. I was to be both conservative and charming and, of course, admire my dear husband in front of his peers.

After I finished my chores, I showered and then laid out his clothes I picked up from the dry cleaners earlier that day. I examined the attire to be sure there wasn't a wrinkle, spot, or flaw present. I didn't need to start the night off on a bad note. I had several ties available for him to choose from that I carefully matched up with his shirt for the evening. His shoes were shined and lined up on the floor for him to easily pick from.

I headed into the bathroom to begin my hair and makeup. I already started feeling a bit anxious as I knew he would be home soon, and I needed to be ready. I hauled ass to get dolled up as fast as I could. I went back into the walk-in closet and started to examine my wardrobe. All of these beautiful things. I could sit in here for hours. Fur coats, bags, and blouses wrapped around the room. The center isles housed my jewelry and smaller accessories. I started to search through my racks of dresses, trying to find options for the evening. Some seemed too short. Others had a deep neckline, and some appeared too tight. As I pushed through the dresses, I noticed my hands were trembling. I grabbed my hands together and held them still. I took a deep breath and tried to calm my nerves. It may seem like a simple thing to get dressed. For me, however, it could be the difference between a bruise or a couple of cracked ribs. I had to choose whatever HE liked, not what I did. I couldn't be an embarrassment in any sense to him. Sometimes, what I thought he would like, he hated, and vice versa.

I kept peeking at the clock; he would be home any minute, and I still had nothing to wear. Every dress I frantically grabbed, I hung right back. I began to panic and felt overwhelmed and nervous. I took another deep breath and continued my search. Here! I forgot I got this a few weeks back. It's perfect. Long-sleeved satin dress, baby blue, with a small slit up the right leg. Just enough to look the part he wanted me to be but modest enough to not draw the attention of anyone else. Nailed it!

I removed my bathrobe and slid into the soft dress. It fit like a glove but had some stretch for it to not be threatening. I stood back and admired myself in the mirror. My long blonde hair lay along the periwinkle shine. It reminded me of the blue skies that hovered the country fields back home. I smiled at myself, proud of the look I was able to pull off. I hoped Ryan would be pleased. The softness of the satin and shimmer of blue made me feel lovely and comfortable. The long sleeves and high neckline gave me a Jackie O feel of glamor and class. Most importantly, of course, they hid my bruises. Always something I have to consider when getting dressed. Hiding the marks. Over the years, he hit me less in my face, as it's easier to cover beatings of the body. Remember, Ryan would never want his image tarnished. I suppose that was the one benefit of his reputation, no flaws are to be seen. Doesn't mean that I never was hit in the face, just not as much as the body. I, of course, mastered the art of makeup and concealer for those days.

I strapped up my Manolo Blahnik's, put on my dangly earrings, and grabbed my coach clutch. I glanced at myself one last time in the mirror to make sure I was up to par. Feeling good and glam, I did one last turn to check for any imperfections. Flawless. I was all set and ready to go, just in time as I heard the front door slam shut.

"Meadow dear, I'm home."

# CHAPTER 5

We arrived at the Waldorf's hand in hand with our everlasting illusion of the perfect couple. Greeted by a hotel staff member, we were taken to our private room for dinner and to meet our guests. As I walked through the hallways, I intensely admired the art and architecture. I had been to this property for numerous events but always was in awe as if it was my first visit. It was a landmark of luxury in Chicago, a symbol of grandeur and success. It featured a Parisian style with modern amenities and lavish decor. As the concierge opened the grand doors leading to our premier dining space, the light radiated from our faces. The glow of the room illuminated the intimate space so warmly and inviting. Chandeliers hung from the high ceilings and reflected off the broad, wood paneling. It was the perfect backdrop to the long table that sat before me. Draped in crystals, elaborate floral arrangements, and countless candles. There were engraved place settings next to our porcelain dinner china. This was incredible; what a vision. The opulent furnishings, roaring fireplace, and the elegant atmosphere were the most perfect ambiance for our gathering.

After graciously greeting those in the room, we took our place at the table. Dinner was exquisite, and the evening was lovely. Ryan was always in a great mood when he was the center of attention and engaged among his colleagues who admired him. After we finished our divine meal, we started to roam around the room, chatting with each other. Everyone was in great spirits, and the evening ultimately was perfect. I found myself relaxed, engaging in conversations, and laughing hysterically. If only it could always be this way. I stood between two Stepford Wives who were raving about their Botox and laser treatments. I just would grin and nod as I was much younger and had not had any of these things done. I didn't care much for the conversation itself but the companionship was what I needed. I turned my head over my shoulder and saw Ryan a few feet behind me in deep conversation with a couple of his partners. He smiled softly at me and even winked. It had been so long since I saw that gleam in his eyes, which radiated among the candles lit throughout the room. I blew him a kiss, in which he let out a small laugh and candidly went back to chatting. Why couldn't he always be this way? I missed this.

I excused myself from the ladies surrounding me to walk over to the bar for another glass of wine. As I stood there waiting for the bartender to pour, I felt a hand placed on the small of my back. I instantly beamed and looked over to Ryan. However, it was not Ryan standing there with his hand on me. It was John York, an investor in Ryan's portfolio.

"Meadow, you are absolutely stunning tonight. This dress is gorgeous."

"Awe, thank you, John. I try to look my best for Ryan. Can't let him show me up." I casually giggled as I moved my body further away from him, attempting to displace his hand from my back. He stood firm, however which made me start to sweat. I knew Ryan was watching and had to get out of this situation fast.

John handed his glass to the bartender, "Another Old Fashion, please, with Angles Envy, good sir."

This allowed him to finally break his grip on me.

"Cheers, John."

I held my glass up towards him as I stepped back to make my exit. He grabbed my hand as I was stepping away.

"It's great seeing you, Meadow. Ryan is a very lucky man."

I placed my head down and subtly nodded, "Thank you."

My face felt flush and I was hot throughout my body. I kept my eyes down as I walked back over to the botox babes, avoiding looking at Ryan. I could feel his eyes burning holes through me. As I took my stance again between the ladies and a couple more who had joined the conversation, I slowly looked back behind me toward Ryan. His eyes were firmly locked on me, but not with the loving gleam that was there moments ago. The twinkle in his eyes was long gone and now replaced with a sharp glare and enraged scowl. This was not going to be good. I smiled at him and turned back to the ladies, acting as if nothing was wrong. *Perhaps if I act not aware of the situation, he will calm down. Wishful thinking has never worked out in my favor, but there is always hope.*

We concluded the evening shortly after that and said our goodbyes to everyone. I didn't want to leave. I knew the wrath was coming. Ryan didn't say anything to me as we stood out front, waiting for the valet to bring the car around. He just stood there, looking straight ahead. I could see the sides of his temple throbbing. He was irate. I kept still and quiet. I did not want to add any fuel to the fire. When the car came around, I thanked the driver and got inside the passenger seat. Ryan slowly walked around the car, before entering. My anxiety was growing more and more, waiting for what he was going to do. I was already thinking of what to say when he questioned me about John. It wouldn't matter though. What I say never matters. I would be punished, most certainly, for my embarrassing antics and behavior as usual. The drive home was the only thing in my favor. Time before we stepped foot in our home, and he beat me again. I never wanted time to move so slowly. I hope we hit every red light on the way. It would at least derail the hitting that will go on in our living room once we arrive.

He didn't speak a word to me the entire way home. He just sat silently and stared straight ahead. I looked out the window, counting down the minutes until the silence would end and his anger would erupt. I gazed at the luxe shops and towering skyscrapers on the Magnificent Mile along the way. Remembering how, when I first moved to this city I was enchanted by this area and all of its glory. High fashion retail, sophisticated salons, gourmet eateries, and breathtaking real estate. The vibrant and posh premier upscale commercial district of Chicago was my favorite place in the entire city. Right now, though, it wasn't enough. I wish it was 30 miles long. That would be magnificent.

We dreadfully arrived home in what felt like seconds. I remained quiet but not sulking, as I didn't want to imply I did something wrong. We entered the house through the garage door and walked inside. As I stepped into the kitchen, I placed my clutch and phone on the island, and I proceeded to kick off my heels. The door shut, and I could hear Ryan moving toward me.

"Take off your dress." He snarled.

"What?"

"You heard me, Meadow. Now, take off your dress."

"Can I at least go into the bedroom to take it off so I can change? Why do I need to take off right this second Ryan? Please don't do this."

"I see. You love the dress so much you just don't want to part with it. Or is that you love the attention you get in the dress more? I'm the only one here now, dear, and I am not a fan of the dress and want it off."

I slowly gulped down the knot that was growing larger and larger in my throat. My heart started to race, and I was trying with all my strength to stop my hands from shaking. I calmly and very casually turned towards him as I reached behind me to unzip my dress. He watched intently and tight-lipped. Gradually, I removed one arm from the sleeve and then the other. The dress fell before me in slow motion. The slick satin that embraced my body and made me feel beautiful now unveiled the battle scars and bruises that hid underneath. My eyes began to fill with tears that I choked back with every bone in my body.

"Look at me, Meadow."

I raised my chin up and looked straight at him. His eyes were sharp and steel, piercing through me as though they were beams of fire.

"I am so sorry, Ryan. I honestly chose this dress thinking you would love it. I didn't mean to upset you. I will go change right now and let's enjoy the rest of the night. The party was so fun and you look so handsome..."

Ryan smacked his hand on the island, interrupting me abruptly,

"Enough! I simply ask for you to show me some respect, especially in front of my partners, and you just can't. Why is it that you love attention from other men? Are you trying to teach me a lesson Meadow? Do you think I don't appreciate you? Why else would I feel the need to dress like that for attention?"

"Ryan, I promise I only want to look good for you and you only. That is never my intention to seek out another man's attention. I didn't approach John, he came up to me and I didn't want to be rude." "I pleaded, with. "Of course, he came up to you, Meadow, look at what the fuck you were wearing? For how much fucking money I spend on your wardrobe, you still manage to look like a cheap hooker. Wait to go."

I picked my dress and heels up off the floor and started to head towards the bedroom. He followed right on my heels as I walked down the hallway and turned into the doorway. I sat my things down on the bed and made my way over to my dresser. He stood in the doorway, arms crossed, watching my every move. I pulled out a T-shirt and sweatpants and slid them on as quickly as I could. I slowly stood up from slipping on my pants when he charged at me from behind. Grabbing me by the back of the neck and slamming my face into the dresser. Blood began to gush everywhere, running from my nose like a faucet. Still grasping my neck, he turned me around, facing the bed, and threw me on it. I fell back, dizzy and disorientated. Before I could gather my bearings, he was on top of me. Straddled across my body, and his hands squeezed my neck tightly. Tighter and tighter, I couldn't breathe. I was pulling at his arms and scratching at the tops of his hands. Desperately trying to get him to release his grip.

"Meadow, you just don't learn, do you? DO YOU?!!!" he screamed at me, spit flying from his manic mode of hatred down on me.

I kicked my legs and tried to get loose. His grasp was too strong, and his hold too tight. This was it; he's going to kill me. With the last bit of fight I had left, I turned my engagement ring around on my finger and dug it as hard as I could into the back of his hand. He let go.

"You bitch!"

He pulled his hand back to hit me again, and just at that moment, I reached out to grab one of my heels. I struck him across the temple with it before his fist could reach my face. He fell off of me, landing on his side beside me on our bed. I hurried up and searched the room frantically for something to hit him with as he was coming for me. There was a glass curio cabinet in the corner. I darted for it just as he was standing up from the bed. I extended my arm and reached into the cabinet for the glass vase on the second shelf. The one he bought me for our 5th anniversary. He gave it to me right after he bruised my left eye for not letting him order first at dinner that evening. Just as I had a solid grip on it, he was moving towards me in a rage of fury from the bed. I sharply turned towards him, a vase in hand, and hit him across the face with every ounce of muscle my small frame housed. He went down.

I stood there for a second in shock and disbelief. Did I kill him? Why isn't he moving? I gently leaned down to look at him closer and that's when he suddenly reached out and pulled my leg. Bringing me down to his level. I swiftly kicked him in the chin, got up, and ran out of the room. I hustled down the hallway as quickly as I could. I just had to make it to the garage, and from there, I was gone. I was trembling with fear, blood-covered, dripping in sweat, and heart pounding. The hallway seemed endless. I felt like I was in The Shining. *Where is the end? Why is everything in slow motion right now? I just need out.*

"Meadow!!!" he screamed for me from the bedroom.

I could tell by his voice he was now upright and coming. I hauled ass around the corner, grabbing my clutch off the island in the kitchen. I quickly turned back and headed to the garage door. We keep our keys on hooks next to the door leading to the garage. It had the keys to all of our vehicles. As I grabbed the keys to my car, I hesitated briefly, looking at the others before me. *He will follow me as soon as I'm out the door.* With that thought, I yanked every damn key off of there and ran into the garage. I slammed the door behind me, grabbed my emergency pack from the cabinet, and hopped in my car. I instantly locked the doors on the vehicle and then hit the garage door opener. I started the car and watched for the door to fully open in my rearview mirror so I could get out of there.

"You're not going anywhere, Meadow. Get out of the car now!"

Ryan was in the doorway, now matching me with blood-soaked clothes and a battered face. He seemed unsteady on his feet, holding himself in the door frame for balance and support. I actually hurt him. I couldn't help but grin just a tad to myself. I'd never seen him vulnerable before. It felt great knowing I put some pain on him for once. However, before I could gloat too much, he was already shutting the garage door on me.

"Get out of the car, Meadow, or I'm dragging you out. NOW!"

*This is it, fight or flight.* I put the car in reverse, hit the gas pedal, and backed right out through that garage door. I've been through hell and was not going to let a piece of aluminum get in my way at this point. I shredded that garage door into pieces, screeched my tires, and pulled out of my driveway with a vengeance. Barefoot, bleeding, and bruised, I peeked into my review mirror to find Ryan wobbling in the driveway, wailing his hands and screaming at me. I exhaled slowly, smiled deeply, turned the radio up, and then drove away fast and furious.

# CHAPTER 6

I knew it would be only a short time before he found the spare keys I hid and came after me. Time was limited, so I had to act fast. I began driving through town to head to the interstate when the low fuel light came on the car.

"Noooo!" I couldn't help but scream out loud as I smacked my hands on the dashboard. "No, no, no, fuck!!"

Ahead, I could see the yellow glow of a Shell gas station sign. I hit the gas and streamlined that way. Just at that time, my phone began to ring, and ring, and ring. Ryan. My heart sank, and my hands slowly began to tremble once again. What am I doing? He's going to find me. He's going to find me and kill me. My mind couldn't rest. Tears rushed through my eyes once again. Although I had ran, I felt as if he still had a grasp around my throat, as it was hard to swallow. I wiped my eyes and pulled into the gas station. I grabbed some cash from my bag and ran inside to prepay. There wasn't a sole in there other than the clerk, yet it felt like hours waiting for her to give me my change. I couldn't breathe, I couldn't think.

"Keep the change," I yelled as I bolted out of the door back to the pump.

I could hear my phone ringing from inside the car as I waited for the fuel to flow. Tapping my foot, pacing back and forth, waiting for it to fill enough to go. Then, silence. My phone stopped ringing. I stood still and listened, but nothing. I removed the nozzle from my car, hung it back on the pump, and jumped in my car.

As I started the engine back up, my phone pinged with a notification. It was a text. It was Ryan.

"Grabbed the wrong car, huh? Need some gas, I see, dear. I'm coming to bring you back home. Honey."

Oh god, he can see my location. He can track me on my phone. Fuck. I didn't think of that. Why didn't I think of that? What should I do? Thoughts raced in my head just as fast as my heart was. I needed clarity. I was in a panic mode and needed to pull myself together. Think Meadow, think. He is coming for you and will keep coming. How do I stop him from coming? I didn't have a moment to think. I had to go. I peeled out of the gas station and headed north, I took the north exit towards Michigan. I wanted to throw him off, knowing he was watching me. I hit the freeway and drove for what felt like forever. My phone began to ring again, over and over. He would call, hang up, and call again. I couldn't take it anymore.

"STOP IT!!!" I shouted at the top of my lungs as I snatched the phone off the passenger seat and threw it out my window.

I began to ball. I cried so hard I could barely see. What am I doing? He is going to find me and kill me. Why did I think I could 'run?' He said he would kill me if I ever left. What am I thinking? That's it. He will kill me if he finds me. If. What if he doesn't find me? What if he can't? That's it, he won't.

Just at that moment, the stars aligned, and the signs were clear. There was an exit ahead, a sign for the Greyhound bus pictured before me. I swerved quickly to the right, hopping the median some to clear the exit ramp in time. As I got off the exit, I could already see a Motel 6 sign ahead of me and a bus pulling into the parking lot. I looked around as I approached the area, this was a dead zone. I stumbled upon some small town, and it was the middle of the night, and no one was around. No one. I pulled off to the right of the road. There was an overpass bridge between myself and the motel with the bus. I took a deep breath, put on my seat belt, and floored it right into the wall of the overpass.

I sat still for a moment, pushing the airbag away from me. Glass was all over me, in my hair, and I had cuts on my hands. I pushed open the door and fell out. Crawling away enough until I could stand. Once I took a second to realize I was ok, I leaned back in the car and grabbed my bag from the passenger side. I dug through it swiftly, grabbing another sweatshirt and swapping it for the one I had on. Then, I grabbed a hair tie from the bottom of the bag, swooped my hair up into a low bun, and placed my long brunette wig on. I threw my bag over my shoulder and walked back to the trunk. Please, please be here. Please. Gasoline: I was looking for gasoline. We had taken the boat out the prior weekend and I remembered we took gas but didn't use it all. I only hope Ryan forgot to get it out.

I closed my eyes and said a little prayer before slowly opening the trunk. Gasoline! It was there, oh my god, it's there. I grabbed it and slammed shut the trunk. Pouring gas from front to back and inside the car as well in a fury. Shit, how do I light it? I needed to go. I had to get to the bus before it left. I needed a lighter or matches. Wait, I needed a lighter. My dad. That's it. My dad's zippo I took when I went home for his funeral. The zippo was his dad's before, and he always carried it after my grandpa passed. It was my favorite thing.

Rugged and beautiful all at the same time, just like my dad was. This was a sign, I see you, Dad. I see the sign.

I reached into my bag and grabbed the lighter. I kissed it, flicked it open, and threw it in the car. The flames rose up and warmed my face. I threw my sweatshirt I had on when I left the house inside the car and ran towards the motel. I didn't look back. I didn't need to. I ran like I'd never run before. The faster I ran, the further the bus seemed to be from me. I kept going, kept running. I peeled around the corner like a child racing to an ice cream truck. As I came up the side of the bus, I slowed down and caught my breath. Deep breaths. I needed to settle down some before stepping on this bus, I didn't want to cause any attention to myself. They couldn't see the car on fire from here, but once the bus pulled out, they would. I took one more breath, fixed my wig, and stepped onto the bus.

The driver looked down at me with a sincere, sweet smile, "Good evening, young lady, come on in." As I began up the steps, her face grin shifted south. "Are you ok honey?" she asked with such deep concern.

She's looking at my face. I hadn't looked in the mirror since I dashed out of the house. My face was covered in blood, and my left eye was swollen almost completely shut.

"Oh, yes, ma'am, I am fine," I bashfully said as I lowered my head in shame and embarrassment. She grabbed a bottle of water from the cupholder in front of her and a few tissues that sat in a box down to the right of her seat.

"Take these honey and clean yourself off. You're safe now."

I grinned and nodded and took a seat in the back. Moments later, the doors shut, lights went low, and the bus pulled out. As we passed my engulfed car, I heard a passenger say, "Wow, I sure hope no one was in that car."

I had to look down during that time, as I couldn't stop smiling. No phone, no car, no Meadow. This will mean no Ryan. I did it. I actually did it. He will never leave another bruise on me. There is no me for him to find. It would look as if I was in such a hurry and speeding off the exit that I lost control of the car. Ryan will know that the gas was in there from the boat and not question it. I did it. I escaped and freed myself. I'm coming home, mom.

I had roughly a 9-hour ride to Lexington, switching buses once. We had some time before the next bus pulled off, so I headed into the gas station to go to the bathroom and grab a snack. Lots of snacks. I was absolutely starving and was not above a greasy gas station hot dog. I came out of the bathroom and browsed the isles, grabbing random carbs and candy. I headed to the cashier to ring up my junk food, there were a couple of people in front of me, so I was waiting with my hands full. I looked around the store, patiently waiting when my attention was forced to focus.

The TV behind the register was playing the news, the news of a car found burnt to a crisp. A tragic story of a young woman who owned the car and didn't survive the crash. It was me. The reporter stated that during the early morning hours, just North of Chicago, firefighters responded to a call of a crash off the interstate and a car submerged in flames. By the time the fire department was able to arrive at the scene, the car had exploded. They were able to salvage plates found a few feet from the vehicle. They were able to get in contact with the owner of the vehicle, who stated his wife had left with the car earlier and verified it did belong to him. The reporter stated how sorry she was for her husband's loss and reminded the public to slow down when driving. Point noted.

I bought my bag of crap food and headed back on the bus. I tried to walk calmly, although I felt like skipping. Why didn't I do this years ago? Never mind that now it's over. All over. I took my seat back on the bus, ate like a prisoner, and then passed out. I slept for hours. It was amazing. Unbothered, relaxed, and refreshed. I woke shortly before we arrived in Lexington. I was so excited knowing how close I was to my mom now. She has no idea I'm coming. I wondered if she missed my morning call today. I call every morning, but not today, for obvious reasons. Will she know me when she sees me? I wondered what shape she was in and how she would react. I was so anxious I was crawling out of my skin to get to her.

It would be about a 25-30 minute drive from her facility to our home in Versailles. I needed a car. I have my mom's back home, but I need it now. I had to transport her and her things back home, not that there would be much, but more than I wanted to shove in an Uber. We entered town, and my heart became overjoyed. I haven't felt excitement and anticipation like this for years. It was truly the best feeling. The driver pulled into our stop, and I stepped down from the steps, landing my feet on the pavement in Kentucky. Home, I'm finally home. I stood there with my bag over my shoulder, scanning the area. This was a metro area, much busier than the last couple of stops. Perfect. I should definitely be able to find a car lot here. I took off walking towards the bustling streets, searching for something.

After about 4 painful blocks of walking, I could see a large American flag waving in the breeze. My eyes followed it down, bingo. A small car lot lay just ahead of me. How symbolic. Car dealerships always have American flags raised, large flags typically. It's supposed to convey the thought that purchasing a vehicle is patriotic, or something like that I've heard. I found it ironic, as the flag represents freedom for me. Following the flag would lead me to freedom, my own car driving me straight to my mother. With a little bounce in my step, I pushed forward towards the lot.

After crossing a few intersections, I entered the dealership lot. Red, white, and blue balloons flew over the cars, ribbons tied to the antennas. I slowly walked by, checking out the used car selection in front of me. So many to choose from, and in all honesty, I didn't give a shit as long as it ran. I made my way over to the SUVs. I needed some room to get my mother in comfortably and load up her belongings. I found myself in front of a 2012 GMC Acadia. Perfect. This will do just fine. I didn't care how many miles were on it, that the paint was chipped around the door frames, or that the tires were pretty beat up. I was also beat up. The car seemed to be a perfect match. I made my way inside, looking for a cheesy salesman in a cheap suit.

However, I was pleasantly surprised to find a very short, old man heading my way. Wearing Wranglers, cowboy boots, and a western shirt with the old snap buttons down the front. My dad always wore shirts like that. Made me think of when he would take me riding. We had matching cowboy hats, and he even got me tassels for my little pink cowboy boots. I had already forgotten that I wasn't in Chicago anymore. This was Kentucky. Old values still stood firm and suits were only worn to funerals.

"How can I help ya miss?" The old man said as he came closer to me.

"Yes, hi, sir. I was interested in purchasing the Acadia you have out front. It's white, sitting straight out to the left."

"Sure thing, dear, let me grab some plates to throw on it so you can give it a test drive. Can I get your driver's license to make a copy while you take it around the block?"

"Actually, sir, I would prefer to just buy it right now. I don't need a test drive."

He looked at me confused and awkwardly, tilting his head slightly to the left and letting out an uncomfortable chuckle.

"Well, miss, that is just fine. Let's come back to my office, and I'll draw up the paperwork and get your information and then can get you going, should take about 30 minutes or so."

I didn't have time for this. It took me six years to get this far. I didn't have 30 more minutes to spare. I took a deep breath and smiled at that man. I lowered my head slightly as I began to remove my sunglasses. I raised my head back up to him, brushing my hair out of my face. The man suddenly looked as though he saw a ghost. Although I had scrubbed off the blood, the bruises were visible, as well as the swollen eye. He looked at me with horror.

"Miss, are you ok?"

"I am now, sir, thank you. But it would really help me out if we could skip paperwork, and I could just buy this car out right and be on my way. Now, that car says $7499 on the windshield. How about I give you $8000 cash, and you just slide me the keys."

He stared at me in disbelief and pity all at the same time. He looked me up and down, looked behind at the car, and then turned side to side to see if anyone else was listening to our conversation. Bob, as his name tag read, gradually raised his hand to his head and removed his cowboy hat. Held it to his chest and nodded his head toward the back office.

"Put your glasses back on and follow me."

My eyes lit up, and I grinned from ear to ear, "Yes, sir."

I placed my sunglasses back on, dropped my chin, and followed him to his office. He led me to a seat across from the cherry wood desk and closed the door behind me. He shuffled through some paperwork until he found the title. As he was searching through the row of keys hanging, I opened my bag and placed the $8000 in cash on his desk. He signed the paper and slid it across the desk along with the keys.

"If you could hold on just one more moment, there is something else I'd like to give you."

He then made his way across the room, where he moved a picture off the wall, revealing a safe, just like in the movies. After placing the combination, he slowly opened the safe door. He reached inside and felt around for a few seconds, looking for something.

"Awe, there it is," Bob grabbed something from the vault and shut the door behind him.

He turned to me and walked over. With his other hand, he grabbed the keys and title off his desk and handed them to me.

"I don't know you, young lady, and I don't need to. Please take this with you, you look like you might need it more than I do. I've had that for years. It might be able to get you out of a jam one day." He grabbed my hand and turned it palm up, then placed a sterling silver pocket knife in my hand. This wasn't a pocket knife you buy from a souvenir shop. This was bigger, heavy, vintage, and beautiful.  I looked down at the gift and wrapped my fingers tightly around it. My eyes teared up, and my heart was full. Kindness, I forgot what this was like.

"Thank you, Bob," I said as I took my things and strutted out the door to my new car. I'm coming home, mama.

# CHAPTER 7

My mom's assisted living home was just 12 miles away from the car dealership. I eagerly headed in her direction when I just happened to glance up into the rearview mirror and see my reflection. Broken and bruised, I couldn't walk in like this. I made a sharp right into the Walgreens parking lot. I parked my car and ran inside, straight for the cosmetics aisle. I loaded up on the concealer and took off. I arrived at her residence and did a quick application of makeup in the parking lot. I grabbed a fresh t-shirt from my bag and brushed through my ratty wig. Good enough, it's showtime. The lady at the front desk was delighted to see me and led me to my mother. I told her I would be taking her home today so bring any necessary paperwork for me while I pack up her things.

I stood outside my mother's door. It was about halfway open. I could see her feet tapping. She must have been in her rocking chair. I could hear, 'The Price Is Right.' Wheel of Fortune playing and just giggled to myself, she always loved that show. We had a small TV in the workshop of Mom and Dad's furniture store. Sometimes, we would have a customer in the building looking for assistance and when I'd look for my mom, I'd usually find her back there. Bidding on the showcase showdown. Some things never change. I slowly pushed the door back further for me to walk through and began to sing quietly.

"You are my sunshine, my only sunshine. You make me happy when the skies are gray. You'll never know, dear, how much I love you..."

Her small, weak voice cried out, "Please don't take my sunshine away."

I fully entered the room, visible to her.

She burst into tears, raising her arms out to me, "My Meadow. My sweet Meadow!"

I rushed to her, falling to the ground on my knees before her. Wrapping my arms around her, kissing her hands, kissing her cheeks, holding her. Crying, laughing, crying more. It was the best day of my life.

"Mama," I said, as I backed away from her still holding her hands tightly, squeezing. "Guess what, mama?"

She looked at me wide-eyed, smiling, "What?"

"I'm taking you home."

"Home? My house? I'm going home?" She was so excited she grabbed me around my neck and pulled me close. "Oh, Meadow, I'm so happy!"

"And I have another surprise for you mom, I'm coming home with you!"

She leaned back, loosening her grip and gently setting her hands now on my cheeks. Tears streamed down her face, and pulled me close once again. After a couple of seconds, she gently pushed me away from her.

"Meadow, what happened to your face, honey? Why is your hair like this?" She pulled lightly on my wig, confirming that it was not my real hair, and then placed her hands on the sides of my face.

Bringing me back into her, kissing my forehead.

"I'm fine, mama, I promise. Just had a bad day. I'm here now, though, and everything is better. Let's get you out of here!"

Her arms relaxed from around my face and she brought her hands to her own face now, wiping her tears. I stood up and held my hand out to help her from her chair. The lady from the front desk walked into the room with a clipboard in hand and another girl beside her holding some boxes.

"Just sign these forms, and this should be enough for all her things," pointing to the boxes the girl    just placed on the chair. "If you need more boxes, just come down to the front desk and let me know. Bye, Mrs. Williams, it was a pleasure having you here. We sure are going to miss you."

The ladies each hugged my mom, and I thanked them as they left the room.

My mom began pulling clothes from the dresser drawer while I ran through her closet and started packing her things. All of the furniture belongs to the facility. She just had her nightstand and pretty much clothes and toiletries. And pictures, she had so many pictures. It made me happy and sad all at the same time. My dad was in nearly everyone, the great love of her life. The only love of her life. I missed him so much and couldn't begin to imagine how much her heart ached for him.

"Meadow honey."

"Yes, mom?" I turned towards and saw her holding a picture of my dad and me in her hand. Stroking the photo ever so gently as she stared deeply at it.

"Is your father at home, Meadow?"

There it was. The good old dementia was rearing its ugly head. Holding back my tears, I forced a smile on my face, "No, Mom, he isn't home right now."

She dropped her shoulders with disappointment and placed the framed photo in the box in front of her with the others, "Well, hopefully, he will be there by supper time."

I agreeably nodded and then went back to unloading the closet. It wasn't much longer that I had her packed up and ready to go. I loaded all of her things in the car and then brought her out. After getting her comfortable in the passenger side, I ran around the car to hop in. She was grinning from ear to ear, looking at me as I started the car and put on my seatbelt.

"Meadow honey, how are you going to stay with me at home? What about your husband?"

I put the car in reverse and grinned back at her, "My husband was my bad day, mama, and I'm not having any more of those."

She nodded and gave me a sweet, sad smile as she reached over and grabbed my hand, "Let's go home, Meadow."

And off we went.

It took about 40 minutes to get home. We drove by a KFC, and she lost her shit, so I had to stop and get her a 2 piece. Evidently the assisted living facility didn't offer drumsticks and biscuits on the regular. We licked our greasy fingers off just as we started coming down the road of our property. I could already see it ahead. My heart started to race, but not with fear as before, but with excitement. Pure and genuine excitement. I slowed down as we began to approach the fence to our yard, well part of it. Our old white farmhouse boosted a wrap-around porch that was our family sanctuary. We spent so many nights out on that porch swinging, looking at the stars, and watching the horses roam around. Back when we had horses, of course. Our property housed a 6 horse stable, a 40x60 pole barn, and 2 other smaller sheds directly behind the house. Just the area to the east of the property was fenced, where the horse stables were. I would fill it again with horses one day.

I turned into our gravel driveway and was homebound. I was mesmerized and enchanted. I was smiling so hard that my cheeks were beginning to ache. I looked over at Mama. She gazed out the window with so much joy. Her eyes wandered the perimeter, examining the property. It was a sight. Her, the house, all of it. I looked right and then left, admiring the property myself. It had been kept up so well. I was so pleased. There was certainly some TLC that needed to be applied, but overall, it was a sight for sore eyes.

Our driveway was lined on both sides with white dogwood all the way to the house. They had just bloomed and were breathtaking like clouds leading the way to heaven right here on Earth. The sky was the brightest blue I'd ever seen, clear and the air clean. The smell of freshly cut grass and a subtle breeze flushed through the car windows. It was quiet and peaceful, everything I desired and needed more than ever. Being cooped up in the city for so long, I didn't appreciate property and space like I do now. Our home was on 14 acres and even had our own little pond. Many of the properties around here did. What I loved about ours the most was it lay adjacent to the west side of the porch. So, if you sat on one side of the porch you could watch ducks waddle in the pond, the other side horses parading around the yard. It was all the inspiration needed for a country song.

"Mama, I'm going to get us some horses again and work on your garden. Would you like that?"

"Oh yes, Meadow, please do!" She held her hands together in her lap, like a child excited to see Santa Claus at the mall. Squirming in her seat looking all around until we finally pulled up to the front door.

I turned to her and grabbed her hand, "Welcome home, Mom."

I hopped out of the car and ran over to help her get out. I held her small, soft hand and led her up the steps. Holding the key in my hand to the front door, I unlocked and slowly opened the door. I felt like I was going to a grand opening for a hotel in the city again. The anticipation and excitement that lay before me, I couldn't contain my enthusiasm.

"Ready, Mom?" I looked over at her, and she was as thrilled as could be. With her eyes open bright, she nodded and grinned.

We entered the front door and stood still as if struck by lightning. Both of us looked around, taking it all in. It had been far too long for both of us.

"Alight, Mom, let's get to work."

And just like that, we went to work. Uncovering all of the

furniture from the dusty white sheets that draped over them. I went around and turned on the lights and opened the windows. It felt so good to be home.

"Hey, Mom, go in your room, and I will bring your things there to put away."

As she headed for her bedroom, and went out and started grabbing her belongings. I came back in, loaded down with a box of clothes, barely peeking over the top to find my way. As I entered her room, I could hear her sobbing. I turned the corner and saw her sitting on the edge of the bed, holding a picture of her and Dad. It was one of my favorite pictures. We had gone camping after the rodeo, and Dad got pretty drunk by the campfire that night. I never heard my mom laugh as much as she did that evening. The photo is her sitting on his lap, giggling uncontrollably while he cheeses behind her, just barely showing his face beside her 90's aqua net hairstyle. Iconic.

"Are you ok, mama?" I asked quietly as I sat the box down and moved closer to her.

"Your dad's not coming home, is he Meadow?"

I placed my arm around her shoulder, "No, mama, I'm sorry he isn't. Do you remember now what happened?"

She cried harder and held her head in her hands, "Yes, Meadow, I do. I do."

I held her while she wept, and she held the photo. After a few minutes of comfort, she raised her head and wiped her face clear of tears.

"Well, let's get the house back in shape like Dad would like. Let's make him proud," she said.

"Oh, he's already proud, mama, but we are going all the way!"

I helped her stand up and then left the room once she was calm again and began to go through the box I brought in.

I unloaded the car, brought everything to her, and helped her get unpacked and settled. I started to make a list for the grocery store. Naturally, there was nothing in the house since it had been empty all this time.

"Mama, I'm going to go to the store here soon. Wanna come with me?"

"Yes, I would love to. Let me just change Meadow, and we can leave soon."

"Sounds good. I'll be in the kitchen when you are ready to go."

I started to go through the pile of mail on the kitchen counter while she freshened up. I began sorting by bills, cards, junk mail, etc. There was also a stack of newspapers so large I figured, this isn't really news at this point, so I began to stack them by the backdoor. They'll make for a good fire later tonight with Mom. As I began tossing them, one at a time, one stopped me in my tracks and took my breath away. I hesitated as I stared at it, pulling it closer to my face to examine it further. It had been so many years since I left, and so much that happened since then I completely forgot about him. Him. Weston Ridge. Right there on the front page, 'Farm Manager of the Year Weston Ridge, The 14 Million Dollar Baby of Versailles.'

I knew he would be something great, something special. Farming was in his blood, so I wasn't surprised. I just hadn't thought of him for so long. I wonder if he ever thought of me. Surely not. Look who he turned out to be. Farmer Joe is a superstar. He's probably married and has a couple of kids. I just kept looking at his photo, his smile. That smile made me weak in the knees even after all of this time. He looked the same as when I left, dashing and handsome but now bigger, stronger perhaps. I could hear my mom shuffling her feet my way, so I gave the paper one last glance and sat it down. On the counter, though, I wasn't going to burn that one. As I placed the article down, I turned to walk out of the kitchen to meet my mom in the entryway. I went to turn off the light and caught a glimpse of myself in the hallway mirror. I stopped and stared once again, but this time at my reflection.

I was a mess. Bruised and broken. I grabbed one of my dad's old Carhartt caps from the coat rack and put on a pair of his aviators. What had I done? I left the golden brick road for the concrete jungle and what did I get, battered and beaten? I had everything I needed right here, and all I wanted was bigger and brighter. The opposite happened, though. I lost my light, my sunshine, my ray of hope and inspiration. The grass is not always green on the other side. Sometimes, it's dead, and that's when you need to get back on your side of the fence. I am here now, no looking back. I took another glance in the mirror and pulled my hat down further to cover my face more.

Pulling open the porch screen door, I looked behind me, "Let's go, Mom."

# CHAPTER 8

We got to the store and I put mom in one of the motorized grocery carts so she could follow along in the store a little easier. We chatted and laughed up and down the isles. There are moments where she gets confused or calls something by the wrong thing, but overall, she still was pretty sharp. And funny, I forgot how naturally funny she always was. I remember being a child and her always dragging me to the grocery store with her. I'd complain and whine at first but then secretly have a fun time shopping with her. She always let me stand at the foot of the cart and would push me through the store. Never say no to me, maybe give me an occasional side eye for whatever junk food I would toss in the cart, but never an actual 'no.' The little things in life we take advantage of, and now I was the one dragging her to the store. It was nice, though, just wandering the aisles. No set agenda, no rules to follow. I had strict orders when I was with Ryan in regard to what I was allowed to purchase or not. Also a limit for shopping, not a spending limit but a time limit. If I was gone longer than an hour, he would call me to let me know he set a timer and the clock was ticking for me to return. I shuddered at the thought of him. It sent chills down my spine.

As we began to wrap up our grocery list and head down to the frozen food section, a lady at the end of the row started waving at us and walking toward my mom.

"Jennifer? Meadow? Is that you?" The lady continued closer, smiling and overjoyed. "Oh my goodness, it's been forever!" She exclaimed as she leaned down to hug my mom.

"Oh, hi, Carol!" I said as I now recognized her. "How are you? It's great seeing you!"

I walked around my cart to give her a big squeeze. Carol Conner was the sweetest woman. She and Mom used to get drunk on the porch off wine in the summers when I was a kid. They had gone to high school together and hung out sometimes. She was always so good to me and my mother. She owned a cute coffee shop in town, too, The Coffee Couture, and we used to go there after school for the best pastries and lattes in town.

I looked down at Mama, "Do you remember Carol?"

I brought my head back up and looked at Carol, "Not sure if you heard, but Mama had a stroke and just gets a little forgetful sometimes."

Carol's smile turned sour as I could see the empathy and heartbreak in her eyes cascading over my mother. She leaned down and hugged Mama again.

"I didn't know, and I'm sorry to hear, but you look great, Jennifer. I wouldn't have been able to tell," she said, squeezing my mom.

"I remember the night you were wasted and fell off the porch swing!" My mom said as she laughed and looked up at Carol and me. There it was. She still had it in there. Of course, that, of all things, is what my mom remembers, but that's why I love her.

After a good laugh from all of us Carol asked what brought me back to town. I told her that I moved back to take care of Mom, not a lie but not the full truth. I wasn't sure if I ever would tell anyone the truth, and I was fine with it. Not talking about it would make it go away faster, and that's all I wanted. For it to all go away. After speaking with Carol for a few minutes, she started talking about her coffee shop and how busy they had been, and that she was short-handed (looking for a new employee and paying cash!) Being back in town and not having a job, I offered to help her out. She was ecstatic with the suggestion and asked that I start that following Monday after getting settled at home with Mom for a few days. It was a great plan, and I was actually incredibly excited. I was not allowed to work. I hadn't worked in years. I only hoped that over the next couple of days, the bruises and swelling on my face would go down more. It's easier to answer the question, 'Why are you back home?' Without a, "battered wife look," on my face. Although I have always dreamed of a career in the fashion industry, this would work for now. I mean, couture is in the title.

## 3 Weeks Later

Life was good. Everything fell right into place, and I couldn't be happier. Mom was doing great, and she transitioned perfectly back into her home. I kept her busy with walks around the property and started her garden back up for her again. I pulled all the weeds out, tilled it up, and got her some new seeds. She was thrilled to be back in her element and had something to tend to. I had been training at the cafe for 2 weeks now, and this morning was my first shift on my own. I loved it! The past weeks had been lovely working in town. Seeing so many familiar faces, past teachers, friends of my parents, and even some of my own class mates. It was refreshening in so many ways. No one questioned my reasoning for coming back. Either they fully believed my sole reason was to care for my mother, or they chose to believe it after seeing the pain in my eyes. However it may be, I wasn't in the position to explain myself to anyone, nor did I have to. Everyone here welcomed me and Mom back with open arms and it was just as if we never left.

I fixed my mom's breakfast, made coffee, and brought her the newspaper before kissing her on her forehead and heading out to open the shop. I looked forward to the drive alone each day to work. Leaving the bustling streets and overwhelming traffic back in the city, this ride was what fed my soul. Passing the horses and cows in the pastures, watching ducks splash in the ponds, and farmers waving you past the combines on the roads. Hometown goodness was full of golden fields and friendly neighbors. The heart of hospitality and my home, I will never leave here again.

I arrived at work excited and anticipating my first day without Carol's oversight. I opened the front door of the establishment and walked in. The baker had been in at 5 am preparing pastries and it smelt sensational in there. The aroma of sugar-filled goodies flooded the room and enticed my nose. I flipped the light switch on and ran my eyes across the room. As I walked about, pulling chairs down from the table tops, I admired the quiet, empty space. I had never been in the store when it was closed. It was so peaceful. The mahogany furniture shone so vividly in front of the Dim light that shimmered through the windows. The shop was intimate and charming. Local artists' work was showcased among the walls, hanging above the tables that lined the interior of the room. Colorful and vibrant boho rugs covered the wood floor and the bar top featured mason jars filled with various flowers, brilliant and bold shades of orange and red. The booths in the back were lined with faux cow fur and created both a cozy and stylish space. The name Coffee Couture was more than fitting for the cafe as it offered soft amenities such as velvet curtains to industrial elements like the metal and wood chandeliers fixed above. I absolutely adored the space. It was a perfect fit for getting back into society and being comfortable. It had been so long since I felt comfortable and safe, confident and secure. I was slowly easing back into it and this helped tremendously.

I flipped on the open sign and unlocked the doors promptly at 7 am. The place was buzzing with customers by 8 am, and things were running smoothly. Old, weathered men gathered around tables telling stories from, 'way back then' and college kids sat in the back booths with headphones on, typing term papers furiously. Farmers flooded in from the fields for a pick me up and the local shop owners popped in through the day as well. It was such a warm and inviting atmosphere. The energy was as contagious as the confectionery. It really was like Cheers, where everyone knew your name.

Once the crowd cleared in the later afternoon, I began to clean up to close. The cafe was open from 7 am to 4 pm, which was great. It got me home just in time to start supper for Mom in the evenings. I brought out my sanitation bucket and rags and made my rounds from table to table, wiping them off and then placing the chairs on top of them so I could sweep and mop next. As I went to sit the tub of water down, I lost my balance and spilt water everywhere. I stood there in despair, looking at the mess I made. Well, at least I was planning to mop next anyway. I headed towards the back closet, through the kitchen, to grab the mop. As I entered the utility room and reached for the mop handle, I heard the bell to the front door ring.

"Just a second!" I yelled from the closet, muffled and distant, not sure if they heard me. Rushing out and closing the door behind me, I ran around the kitchen to come back out to the dining area, mop in hand. The glare from the afternoon sun made it difficult to see who was standing in the doorway. I could only see the silhouette of a man in a cowboy hat with his hands in his pockets.

"Hi, sorry! Did you need something to go, or were you looking to grab a seat? I'm getting ready to close, but you are more than welcome..."

My voice went quiet as I approached the front door. I stopped dead in my tracks, stunned and still. The mop handle fell from my fingers, making a loud crashing sound as the metal pole smacked against the wood floor. It was as if the world suddenly paused.

"Hi, Meadow Weston. So it is true."

It was Weston Ridge. The Weston Ridge, living and breathing right before my very eyes. "Let me get that for you."

He walked over to the broom and gently picked it up from the floor and brought it to me. It was as if someone hit me with a freeze machine, and I could physically not move. The only way I knew I was actually still alive was due to my heart feeling as though it could beat right out of my chest any second now. His cologne seduced my nose. What on earth was that sexy smell? Was it cologne, or was it just him? Good lord, he smelt so good. His head was tilted somewhat down as he was looking at the broom while coming towards me. The brim of his hat was covering most of the face, I could just barely see his chiseled jawline. Although he was only a couple of feet from me, it felt like there were miles between us. Everything was in slow motion. Was this really even happening?

"Here you go," he said as he stood before me with the mop and now raised his head so I could see his face.

It was him, it was really him. He was even more beautiful than when I left. Rugged and sexy, shaved but with a 5 o'clock shadow that I found irresistible. He was bigger and broader. Tan and dirty from working in the field, jeans ripped, and boots stained with dried mud. I reached out to take the mop handle from him, as I was still trying to regain my speech at this time. As I went for the mop, I couldn't help but notice his hands. Those were man's hands. Living in Chicago, it had been years since I had seen real man hands. Not those who type on a computer or even those who smack around women, those who work hard all day in the field. Man's hands can operate machinery, herd cattle, cook ribs, and comfort you until infinity. My dad had "man" hands, I can still remember how they felt when he would touch my face. I missed those hands and that man.

"Thank you," I finally muttered as I looked up into his glistening eyes and melting smile, taking the mop and leaning it against the wall next to me. I opened my arms and reached out for a hug, "it's so good to see you, Weston."

"You too, Meadow!" He put his arms around my waist and subtly pulled me into his body, holding me close to his chest. Embracing me tightly, warmly. He towered over me. His large hands held my back entirely. His smell was intoxicating, and I could feel his heart beating through his shirt. "How are you?"

I leaned back just enough to look at him when speaking, but he still was holding my waist very securely, "I'm good, just came back a couple of weeks ago to take care of Mom. She's been in Lexington at an assisted living facility but now back at home."

"That's great. Did your husband come back with you, too?" I slowly pulled away and pushed my hair back behind my ears, which had fallen out of place. I also tend to do this action when I feel awkward, as I did with this very question.

Looking down at my feet, I whispered no just as my eyes burst into tears. What was wrong with me? I hadn't seen Weston in 6 years, and within 6 seconds, I was already balling. What a mess. He grabbed me again and drew me into his arms.

"I'm so sorry, Meadow," he said under his breath as he stroked the back of my head and ran his fingers ever so softly through my ponytail. "Want to talk about it?"

I pushed away from him and wiped my face. Shaking my head back and forth and taking in a deep breath. I smiled and looked up at him, "No, no, thank you. I am going to be just fine. Please ignore that. Just a transitional period is all I'm working through right now. But it's great to be back home, and Mom is so happy!"

"That is wonderful, Meadow. I'm so happy to see you. I heard from some of the guys you were working up here, so I had to come see for myself."

"Well, now that you've seen it for yourself, what do you think?" I chuckled to him as I grabbed the mop.

Weston looked me up and down and took a deep breath, "I think

I'm one lucky man."

I felt myself start to blush, I smiled cautiously and took the mop back into the kitchen. "I'm getting ready to close up Weston. Is there something you'd like to take to go?"

"Yeah, I'd like to get one thing if you don't mind."

"What's that?" I said, leaning over the counter with pen and paper in my hand.

He reached up and pulled off his cowboy hat, steadily placing it on the countertop. Leaning in and resting his forearms on the countertop, a smile stretched across his face, "I want to take you to dinner."

I threw my head back and laughed, "That is not on the menu, sir." I turned and grabbed the broom from the closet, and shut off the coffee pots. My face was so red I had to step away from the counter and get my smile under control. What am I feeling right now? I can't believe he really wants to take ME to dinner. Why isn't this stud already married? Just breathe, Meadow, breathe. I walked back to the counter and leaned in, still waiting on an actual order.

"Well, it was worth a try. I'll let you close up Meadow, but still would really like to take you to dinner."

"I do appreciate it, but I need to get home to my mom and check on her. I have to make her dinner and help her with her shower. Thank you, though."

"It's not a one-time offer," he reached across the counter and grabbed my hand. "It was really nice seeing you."

"You too, Weston," he grabbed his Stetson from the bar and walked out into the sunset, just as cowboys do, of course.

After he walked out of the door, I stood there in a trance for a few moments. Stunned by the entire interaction. I actually had butterflies in my stomach, I haven't had a feeling overcome me like this for years. I slowly shook off the flutters and went to finish cleaning up. As I grabbed the last few dirty coffee cups off the counter, I reached over to pick up the menus. Just as I was wiping them off one by one and stacking them in a pile, I noticed something. Right under the latte flavors was something written, some kind of scribbled ink. I pulled it closer to read it clearly and then began to blush once more. It read, 'Dinner with Weston.' Evidently, it was on the menu.

# CHAPTER 9

I got home from work that evening to find Mama sitting on the porch swing, sipping sweet tea. Such a wonderful thing to come home to. After a couple of hours of chores, I took a shower and then helped mom with hers. I just stand outside the shower doors to make sure she doesn't slip, getting in and out. I had brought the menu home and showed it to Mom, she got a chuckle out of it.

"That Ridge boy has always been in love with you, Meadow. He asked about you every time I saw him after you left. He's only had a few girlfriends. I think he always hoped you'd come back."

"Stop it, mama," I giggled. "I do not believe that. He can have any woman he wants. He's just being nice."

"No, Meadow, I'm serious. I know I have trouble remembering some things but this I know. They asked him to be on that show, the Bachelor, did you know that? And he turned it down."

"Really?" Of course, they asked him to be on The Bachelor. This beautiful man should be in Hollywood, not in the hills of Kentucky.

"Yes, really, now go to dinner with that poor boy."

I started laughing, "Mom, I'm just not ready to date anyone. I feel like I'm in this weird phase, and I don't know what I should be doing, really."

"Listen, Meadow," she pulled me close and placed her hands on my shoulders. "You have one life, one shot to get this right. You've wasted years with someone who didn't appreciate you. All I'm saying is, I wouldn't waste any more time."

I reached up and grabbed her wrist on each side, smiled, and looked right at her, "I love you, Mama. Now let me cook dinner!"

We both laughed, and I headed towards the fridge while she took a seat at the bistro table in the kitchen. She always sits there and talks to me while I cook. It's my favorite part of the day. When I was a little girl, I would sit there playing with my Barbies or My Little Pony and tell her about the day at school while she made us dinner. The role change I think, is what was most endearing and ironic. I loved tending to her. She took such great care of me and my dad I was more than happy to turn the tables.

Just as she settled into her spot at the table and I was purging the fridge and cabinets to find something to whip up, the doorbell rang. I looked over at Mom, "Are you expecting anyone, Mama?"

She shrugged her shoulders, "No, dear."

I made my way over to the window and slowly peeled the curtain back just enough to look out. There was a silver Tesla in the driveway, not really typical around this area. Odd. Oh my god, it's Ryan. He found me. My heart started to pound, I could feel my throat tightening up, and my hands began to sweat. The doorbell rang again. What should I do? How did he find me? There is no way for him to think I would be here. I crept closer to the door, barely placing the heels of my feet down, treading lightly to the peephole. I stretched my upper body as far out as I could to see out without stepping too close to the door where they could hear me. Placing the palms of my hands gently on the door, trying to control my shaking and stand firm, I looked through the glass ring to the porch.

Ubereats. It was food delivery. I almost had a heart attack. Calm down Meadow. I let out the biggest breath and fell flat to the door. Laughing uncontrollably. Wow, that almost killed me. I composed myself and swung open the door, "Hi, can I help you?" I asked the delivery guy since we had not ordered anything from anywhere. I assumed he was lost.

"Yes, I have a delivery for Meadow Williams. China Hut?"

"That's odd. I am Meadow, but I didn't order anything."

"I know, ma'am, it was called in by a Weston Ridge. He asked for it to be delivered here."

I grinned and nodded my head, "Of course he did." I laughed and reached out to accept the food. "Thank you so much. Have a good night."

"You too, ma'am."

I closed the door, walked into the kitchen, and sat the giant bag of food in front of Mama, "Well, Mom, how does Chinese sound for dinner?"

She smirked at me, "Sounds like you should invite someone over for dinner." And she tossed the inked up menu to me that I brought home, 'Dinner with Weston.'

I lowered my head and chuckled, "Fair enough, Mama, fair enough."

I texted Weston a picture of the menu where I had written 'yes' underneath his request and another photo of the Chinese food. He was at my front door in 12 minutes.

Sitting in my mama's kitchen, eating with her and Weston, made me feel like I was in high school again. I laughed so hard I nearly peed my pants. Mom was going on and on, telling amazing stories from our childhood. So many things that I had forgotten about. I cherished these moments when she spoke with such clarity and intent you would have never known she had early dementia. It was almost as if having Weston there made it better. The doctor did say short-term memory would be more of a challenge for her than those events that occurred before the stroke. Perhaps him being there triggered those memories from the past, creating a comfortable feeling where she felt present. I know having him there made me feel comfortable. It was crazy how we just clicked after all this time. He was so well-mannered and charming, too. Just the little gestures he does are somewhere so grand, and he doesn't even realize it. I was so content at this very moment that I didn't want it to end.

We sat at the table for about an hour after we finished our food, drinking coffee and chatting more. Weston talked to us about his work and family and the projects he and his brothers had done and were currently doing. He was so humble and kind, so successful, and yet remained so modest all this time. The world needed more Weston's. After I noticed my mom yawn a couple of times, I suggested I help her to bed to get to sleep. When I came out from the room I saw Weston placing his hat on his head and standing up from the table. Wait, is he leaving? I wandered back into the room and towards the table. He stopped me as I was entering the doorway.

"Meadow, do you want to sit on the porch with me?"

I grinned and looked up at him, "Weston, would you like to drink some wine with me?"

We both burst out with laughter.

"Yes, Meadow, I would love to."

I walked around him and grabbed a bottle of Chateau Ste. Michelle Riesling from the fridge, two glasses from the wine rack, and motioned my head towards the door, "Well, come on then, big boy."

He cackled and followed behind, then reached ahead of me to open the door.

"After you, Miss," he laid out his arm before me, guiding me through the door.

I waltzed over the porch swing, planted myself down firmly, and set the glasses to the right of me on the wicker table. I placed the bottle of wine in between my legs as I needed my hands free to throw my hair up in a messy bun. Weston closed the door behind him and walked towards me. He stared intently at me, it was as if I could feel his eyes. Not the same way Ryan stared at me. His was an intimidation factor, a sign of anger or disappointment. A warning that some punishment was coming soon. Weston was different. I loved how he stared at me. It was warm and friendly, sexy if I'm really being honest here.

"May I?" Weston said as he reached down to grab the bottle from my lap.

I nodded and grinned and shifted my eyes towards the glasses beside me. He filled them up and then took a seat next to me. It was beautiful out, the stars vibrant and bright, stretching across the black sky. The moon was perfectly placed over the pond, penetrating it with light that glowed immensely. It was so quiet, so peaceful.

"Thank you for dinner, Weston. That was very thoughtful of you."

"You are very welcome. Thank you for accepting the new menu item so graciously," he laughed. "Now what?" He asked.

"Now what, what?" I replied.

Chuckling, he answered, "What are you going to do now, now that you're home?"

"Just take care of Mama, really. I'd like to get some horses again eventually, can't really do that on my wages at the cafe," I joked. "But one day, I'll get there."

"Ahh, yes, you used to love to ride. I can help you get horses. Just let me know when."

He made everything so easy, so simple.

I grinned over at him and clanked my glass to his, "Deal."

We talked for what felt like hours under the gazing moonlight, softly rocking back and forth on the swing. Reminiscing of our school days and early romance. It was the most fun I had in years. As I poured the last of the wine from the second bottle into Weston's glass, he grabbed my wrist and looked at me wide-eyed.

"Are you going to go back to Chicago?"

I almost dropped the wine bottle when he said that. He caught me so off guard.  Just hearing Chicago made my mind race and anxiety skyrocket. I immediately began to shake my head no and gulp down a drink of wine to clear my throat and calm my nerves.

"I don't mean to upset you, Meadow. I'm sorry."

Clearly, he noticed my reaction as I am incapable these days of being discreet with my emotions.

"No, no," I said as I waved my hand towards him. "It's not you at all! Sorry, I'm just still adjusting, I guess. But to answer you, no, I will not be going back to Chicago. Ever."

"Can I ask why? What happened to your husband? I do believe you are here to help your mom, but I don't buy that's the only reason. I know you. You wanted to live in Chicago for years, work in fashion, so it's hard for me to believe you chose to come back and work at a coffee shop.."

"I'm just not ready to talk about it yet, Weston. Nothing went to plan and everything went to hell from there. Not much more to say."

"I'm sorry, Meadow, you just seem like something is wrong. You used to be so relaxed, so free. You seem like you're holding something back or hesitating before you speak. It's just different. I just want to make sure you are ok."

He's right. Who am I fooling? I don't know why I refuse to talk about it. I guess because, for years, I've been scared to talk about it. I had one friend, no family, no coworkers, and no one in Chicago I could turn to or trust, for that matter. Celeste was so sweet, my dear friend who I miss so much. I wish I could call and tell her I'm ok but it's too risky. If Tom would overhear us speaking or she would slip up, I'd be done. I'd be dead. I need to recognize I'm safe now and put it all behind me. I'm just so torn by being embarrassed by what has happened and letting it out so I can heal. Heal my heart and even my body. My body, my poor body. I had so many scars and marks from him. Still, a few bruises left behind that haven't healed fully yet.

I looked over at Weston and nodded slowly. He was right; I am not the same. My eyes began to water as I took a deep breath. I stood up from the porch swing and took one step forward, where Weston was now sitting behind me. I began to gradually raise the back of my shirt up, more and more, until I could feel it had reached my bra strap. Then, I stopped. I just stood there with my back open and visible to Weston. Vulnerable and undeniably awkward, but it's the answer he was looking for. There is something wrong with me, this. The damage done by my husband. The reason I ran and am here. Maybe it was too difficult or too soon to talk about, so all I could do at that moment was just show him.

I could hear him rise up from the swing and step towards me. The boards on the porch creaked as he edged closer behind. He leaned over me and gently ran his fingers over my back. Almost as if he was tracing by scars, following them in a line. He then gradually moved his hand higher until he had a grip on the bottom of my shirt. He began to tug lightly, lowering it back down. Being incredibly cautious as if trying to prevent the material from rubbing against me. I glanced over my shoulder back at him.

"It's ok, it doesn't hurt anymore."

"Oh, Meadow, I wish I knew. I would have come and got you in a heartbeat. I'm so sorry."

"No, Weston, it's not your fault at all. If anyone's, it's mine, I missed every red flag thrown at me until they were smacking me straight in the face. I was blinded by everything around me and in front of me to see what was really happening until I was trapped," I turned back towards him, adjusting my shirt further. He pulled me in and hugged me, close and snug.

"Will   he come to find you here?"

"No, he thinks I'm from Lexington and that Mom and Dad both passed. After he got mad at me for coming home for Dad's funeral, I told him Mom didn't survive her stroke. I knew I'd come back to her one day and didn't want him to have any reason to follow."

"That's smart and sad at the same time he said," looking into my eyes, so concerned and so heartfelt. "How did you get out?"

"We were in a fight, and I ran out and crashed my car so he would think I also didn't survive. I threw out my phone, and Carol was paying me cash at the cafe, so I couldn't be traced by my social security number. I basically disappeared as far as he's concerned."

"Oh my god, I can't believe you've been dealing with all of this. Are you sure you are ok? Do you need to see a doctor or talk to someone?"

"Tonight was the best therapy I could get, and it came with Chinese food," I said as I stepped back from him with a smirk.

He laughed as we sat back down on the swing. He put his arm around my shoulders, and I laid my head back so it rested on his arm. This was nice. We sat quietly just rocking back and forth for a few more moments. I was soaking it in, the comfort, the conversation, and the confession. It felt good to tell my secrets to someone, to get it off my chest and know someone is aware of why I'm not myself. Maybe this same person can help me find myself again.

"What if he figures it out, Meadow, and comes back for you?" Weston asked as he squeezed my shoulder. "What will he do?"

I closed my eyes to the thought, took a deep breath, and looked over at Weston, "Kill me."

# CHAPTER 10

I slept like a baby that night after Weston left, better than I had in years. Maybe it was the two bottles of wine or the confession of my soul; either way, I was rested for once. About a week had passed since my 'Dinner with Weson,' and he would visit me every day at the coffee shop. My heart would skip a beat every time I'd see him strut inside that door; I looked forward to it each day. He was always so happy and delightful to be around. His laugh was infectious, and his demeanor provocative. Was he aware of how sexy he was? Even how he drank his coffee turned me on. Perhaps it was his big hands cupping the little porcelain dish. Or the way his veins bulged out of his forearms when he rested his elbows on the counter. The way he would wink at me across the room and give me that dashing smile would make me feel like I was going to faint. I was transfixed by him more and more each time I saw him. I couldn't get enough. He made my day bright and my heart happy.

"You have a comment box or something around here, Meadow. I'd sure like to give a review today," Weston joked as he was paying his tab. Being cute and looking left and right under the counter for such a thing.

"Haha, funny guy. No comment box around here, farmer joe."

"I see; well, how do I show gratitude for the fine service from the fine waitress I had?"

My face lit up like a Christmas tree; this man could seriously make me blush. I just giggled and shrugged my shoulders as I handed him back his change.

"Keep it," he said as he pushed the money back towards me.

"It's a hundred?"

"Yeah, life's good," he chuckled. "Now, since I can't leave a review, how about dinner? I know it's not on the menu, but if you'd be so kind as to indulge me, I'd appreciate it."

"Well, what about mama?"

"I'll bring mama some more Chinese food when I pick you up for dinner; she will be just fine."

I grinned, "you just have an answer for everything, don't you?"

"Something like that," he said as he flashed a smile and stood up from the counter. "See you at 6 Meadow."

I had a few hours left of work after Weston left, including a late afternoon rush that filled my tip jar. It was a good day, and I couldn't wait until tonight. I enjoyed being around Weston so much; he made me laugh and allowed me to relax. No expectations; he truly seemed to enjoy me for me. Just how I am and what I offer, no more and no less. I started to grow more and more attracted to him. I had a few dirty dreams, and I woke up dripping in sweat. We talked every day but nothing further. I wonder if he was attracted to me; I mean, he makes little comments and gestures occasionally, but is he just flirting harmlessly, or is something there? Was I even ready for anything if that was the case? But what would I even be waiting for? I spent 6 years trapped, beaten, and bruised. I didn't want to waste any more time; life is short, and I've missed so much. Time is the greatest thief; I didn't want it to steal any more than it already had.

Right before I began closing up, Carol, the owner, popped into the shop.

"Hey, doll! How was the day?" She asked as she bounced in with her bubbly self and headed behind the counter to give me a hug.

"It was great!" I answered, leaning in to hug her back. "It's always great, though. I love working here. Thank you so much for giving me this job. I really needed it."

Her smile seemed to slip away as I was saying this to her. I could tell something was wrong.

"I'm so happy to hear that, Meadow, but I do have some news to share with you. I've had this shop for 30 years and loved every minute of it, but I'm getting older and have decided to retire."

I was in shock; this place was my comfort and joy; what would I do now? I just now started to get some cash saved up. I couldn't go anywhere else for a job. I needed to remain in hide-out mode a little longer. I was scared to death of having to use my license or social security card for anything. What if Ryan was looking for me? He is legally my husband and has rights and access to my information. This couldn't be happening right now. I needed this.

"Oh no, Carol, I'm sorry to hear that. I enjoy working here so much, and with my situation, it really is the best fit. Are you closing the shop entirely or looking to sell it?"

She looked at me with empathetic eyes, " I know, dear, I know. I have thought greatly about you over the last couple of days as I finalized this decision. I am going to initially try to sell the business and building as one to someone. That is my goal and hope; that way, the community can still enjoy this place, and YOU will still have a job. This isn't going to happen over night, so just relax, and I promise I will update you along the way. Simply wanted to give you a heads up dear, on what was happening."

"Thank you so much for everything, Carol; I understand and appreciate you letting me know." She gave me a tight squeeze, made herself a caramel latte with nonfat milk, and scooted out the door. After she walked out the door, I finished closing up and hurried home for my 'Dinner with Weston.' I wasn't going to let the news ruin my evening, and like she said, it won't be over night. It's out of my control for the time being, so I just have to brush it off.

Weston arrived promptly at 6 pm with Chinese food in hand and two batches of a dozen roses, one for me and one for mama. This guy was too much. God really molded the perfect man with this one. My mom was tickled pink and elated by the kind gesture and ran into the kitchen to get vases.

"Well, you sure know how to make an impression there, cowboy," I said as I walked up to Weson and gave him a hug.

"Wow, Meadow, you look beautiful." He stared at me with a sly grin, looking at me from top to bottom. He was enchanted and mesmerized. I hadn't been looked at like that for years. I felt good; it felt great. I felt sexy and radiant, comfortable in my own skin, and seemingly confident more and more each day. I have to admit, though, that I made some special effort for this dinner. I glammed up for the first time since I'd been back home. Full makeup consisting of black mascara, shimmering bronzer that made my skin glow like the sun, and popping pink lip gloss that made my lips slick and pouty. I used a liquid eye liner to make my blue eyes vibrant and smokey. It was refreshing to put on makeup just to look pretty as opposed to covering up a bruise. It was fun and made me feel good. I used my beach wave curling iron to get some bounce and texture in my blonde strands. I found my old cowboy boots in the back of the closet and cleaned them up. I paired my tan Tecovas with a red and white floral sundress that hit slightly before my knees. The upper body fit tight like a glove, low cut and exposing a large amount of cleavage. The bottom of the dress flared out and was trimmed with frills. The power to dress how I want is something I have taken for granted; no one is judging me or controlling me now. I can be myself, wear what I want, and do what I want. All I wanted to do right now was go to dinner with Weston.

I grinned and curtsied, holding out the bottom of my dress and dipping my head down. "Thank you, Mr. Ridge."

He laughed, "you're a trip, Meadow. I love it."

We walked into the kitchen, and both hugged mom bye and headed out the door. I was so excited, but kind of nervous too. I wasn't sure if this was an actual date or just dinner with a friend. I felt like there were some signs that he liked me, but now I am kind of worried he may just pity me. Maybe I shouldn't have told him about Ryan and what happened. Perhaps the marks on my back turned him off. Should I have shown him? I'm thinking about this too much; I'm an overthinker and always have been. I brushed off my moment of insecurity and hopped up in his truck. This was a full-circle moment for me. Another F-150 with Weston in the driver's seat, taking me out on the town. I felt like old times; it felt right, it felt good. This one, of course, was brand new, black,  and fully loaded, still with a lift kit naturally. No matter how much money this man has, he is still a country boy at heart. I loved that about him.

"So where are you taking me, cowboy?" I teased as we headed down the drive and out onto the county highway.

"Well, I decided to go for something more intimate. You're at the coffee shop all day, surrounded by the locals, especially those old man fans you have." He laughed, "I thought you might like something where it's just the two of us."

"Oh, ok, I like this idea. But Weston, what restaurant would we be alone at?"

"Hold tight, you'll see." He reached over and grabbed my hand as he turned and winked at me. There are those flutters again, just his touch made me quiver. Everything he did, everything he said, was so effortlessly sexy.

After driving for about 10 minutes, we turned down a country road; it was pitch black and slightly narrow. Wait, this looks familiar. I've been here before. Just as I was looking around to get my bearings and try to remember how I knew this area, I saw it. Weston's home, his childhood home. Where we spent hours among hours sitting by the pond, hanging out on this tailgate, laughing and snuggling. I beamed with joy as we pulled into the driveway, and the memories rushed to my mind.

"My parents moved to Florida a couple of years ago, so I moved into the old homestead. I didn't want to sell it; there are too many memories here." He said as he revealed a sly smile, driving towards the house.

"Oh my god, yes, Weston! This is amazing; we had such good times here."

"This was the last place I saw you before you left. I never thought I'd be able to bring you back here one day." He looked over at me with a gaze in his eye, almost as if he was going to cry. "I've literally wished for this day, Meadow; thank you." He reached over and grabbed my hand again, but this time lifting it to his mouth and gently kissing the top of it.

My heart, oh my heart. I couldn't believe what I was hearing. I wondered if he ever thought about me after I left, and he did. I was always looking forward, young and naive, trying to make my footprint in the world. All along, I had broken his heart, the one heart that beat just for me. I wish I could turn back time, stay here, and be with him. What would my life be like now? Maybe if I stayed here, my mom wouldn't have ever had a stroke, having me near so she wasn't so overwhelmed. I could have taken over my parents' furniture store so it wouldn't have closed. I could have lived at home and maintained the property. We would still have horses. If only. But I couldn't; there was no turning back the clocks. It was what it was, and I'm here now, right here, where I should be. That is all that matters.

"Weston, thank you for this." I smiled and squeezed his hand, bringing it down and placing it on my lap. Holding it while he drove us to our VIP seating. As he crept up the drive to the house, he slowly began to turn left for the path down to the pond. As we approached, I saw a white tent in the distance with tiki torches placed along the corners, illuminating it with a soft glow. I started to beam with excitement at the site. It was all so magical. The pond was lit with Chinese lanterns floating among the surface, radiating so much brightness that the water appeared to sparkle. It was lovely and enchanting, whimsical, and romantic. It was a date. My wandering and curiosity faded along with my concerns and insecurities. He did this for me. For us. He's been waiting 6 years to do this. I was the lucky one now.

Although it felt as if my breath had been taken away, I was able to softly mutter out, "Oh, Weston, this is beautiful."

He held my hand tighter and grinned as we pulled up outside of the tent. Racing out of the truck, he ran around to open my door and help me down. "This way, darling," he said with a southern twang in his tone as he led me inside the tent. Where, once again, he took my breath away. This was surreal. Inside the intimate tent sat a small, round wooden table and two patio chairs. On top of the table laid a lace and burlap table liner. The table was set with his mother's porcelain dishes and 2 crystal wine glasses, along with silverware and napkins. This was the cutest thing I've ever seen. He made our own little restaurant right here on his little piece of the earth, just for us. Candles lined the inside of the tent, bringing an irresistible glimmer to Weston's eyes as he looked over at me from across the table where we were taking our seats.

"Weson, this is incredible! You did all of this for me?" I whimpered as I looked into his eyes with endearment; I was captivated.

"Yeah, look at this." He held out his hands to me and flexed his thumbs back. "See here and over here. I burnt myself doing all this interior decorating. I hope you do like it." He laughed and wrapped his hands around mine, gripping them. "It was all worth the cause," he winked, and we both chuckled.

As we began to chat, two men entered the tent dressed in black dress shirts and pants, one with a bottle of wine and the other with two dinner salads. "You hired butlers for this evening? Wow, you really go out to impress a girl!" I giggled and held my wine glass out for butler "one" to fill. It was a full-course meal featuring a perfectly cooked prime rib topped with sauteed portobello mushrooms, cheesy garlic au gratin potatoes, and roasted asparagus wrapped in bacon. It was phenomenal—the meal, the service, the atmosphere, and mostly the man. 'Dinner with Weson' easily beats anything else on the menu.

# CHAPTER 11

We ate a fabulous meal in our own waterfront private establishment, surrounded by an eminence glow that lit our tent up with a seducing ambiance. It was picture-perfect. We talked and laughed and shared stories and memories. I told him about what Carol had said in regards to selling the business and my concern about how that would play out and where it would leave me.

"Do you really like working there, Meadow? I love seeing you so happy, but I know you wanted a career in fashion; why don't you try to pursue that now that you can?"

"You know, I really do like working there. I actually love it. It is not at all what I thought I would want to do or have a passion for, but nothing in my life at this point went according to plan. I'm actually fine with that, content really.  I love chatting with the regulars every day and being part of the community. It's great how close it is to home, so I can be there for mom if she needs me. I feel important there, comfortable, safe. Maybe one day I can work for Vogue, but right now, this is all I want."

He smiled sweetly at me, "That all makes sense, Meadow; I love that you feel safe and comfortable. That is how you should always feel, and I agree, you are definitely loved there."

"Well, it's nothing I'm going to stress about right now. What's meant to be will be, so we shall see!" I said as I held my glass towards his, initiating a toast.

"Cheers, Meadow, to what is meant to be." Our glasses clinked together, and we sipped down our Meiomi wine while the butlers cleaned our dishes from the table. "Wanna take a walk with me?" He asked as he extended his hand across the table.

"Let's go cowboy." We headed out of the tent as the guys began to clear the space out and pack it up in a trailer that sat behind. We strolled around the pond, wine glasses in hand and stars shining immensely from above. About an hour had passed when the wind started to pick up, and the slight chill in the air turned brisk and cold. "Wanna come back to my house and hang out for a bit? Mama's probably sleeping, we could finish this bottle of wine and make a fire out back?"

"Sounds perfect; since our place is closing up here, we might as well go to the after-party." We both laughed and headed back to the truck, grabbing another bottle of wine from the cooler before the butlers hauled it off with the rest of the load.

We got back to my house and ran in, giggling like two kids in a high school trying to be quiet and not wake Mama. I tiptoed across the wooden planks down the hallway to peek into Mom's room, just as I figured she was sound asleep. I pulled her door shut softly and closed it all the way. I headed back out towards the kitchen and could already see Weston through the window building a fire out back. Suddenly, I thought of something I had found when I was cleaning the house. I laughed to myself and walked over to the pantry door. On the very top shelf, where I had to stretch my short frame to max capacity to reach it, was a little tin jar. It used to be Dad's; it sat on his dresser for years. I always wondered what was in it. Maybe an ancient Indian arrowhead, or maybe ashes of his grandfathers. It had to be something special and significant, but I never knew until just a couple of weeks ago when I opened it for the first time ever. Pot. It was pot. My dad had a stash of joints in what I thought was some treasure chest. Go figure. Anyway, finder's keepers, I grabbed the metallic box and headed out to Weston.

"Guess what I found..." I said, dangling the container in front of Weston's wide eyes.

"Hmmm, what is that, Meadow?"

I tossed it to him and watched him cautiously open it as if a can of worms was going to fly out at him.

"Like old times, Mr. Ridge, wanna spark it?"

"Hell yeah, I do! Oh my god, I haven't smoked since I was with YOU. Ya, little rebel. I should have known your dad was a stoner, the most laid-back guy I ever met."

"Right??!!" I said, "It totally makes sense now!"

We lit it up and sat by the fire, drinking our second bottle of wine and chiefing like Willie Nelson. Weston turned the radio on in his pickup so we had some background music to add to the ambiance as well. The late-night air was cool and crisp; the setting was ideal for the blaze. The rays from the fire made Weston's face shimmer across from me, brilliantly captivating his sexy silhouette. Sparks cascaded around us from the flames flickering among the logs. The bonfire warmed my body and soothed my soul. Country campfires are the best. The cool breeze at my back, radiating heat before me, and thousands of twinkling stars above set the scene for a perfect evening.

"I wanna dance."

"What?" Weston looked up at me, confused, "You wanna dance, like now?"

I giggled and held my hands out to him, "Yes, I do. Can I have this dance, Mr. Ridge?"

"I'd be honored," he said, taking off his hat and setting it in the chair next to him, then taking my hand. We walked over in front of the truck; we snickered as we were both a little unsteady on our feet from the weed and wine. We gained our balance and managed to contain our hysteric roars enough for him to wrap his hands around my waist as I draped my arms around his neck. We swayed back and forth with the glow of the moonlight beaming down on us. I didn't want this night to end. He dipped me, twirled me, and held me close. We circled around each other in our cowboy boots with the grass at our feet. Not your typical dance floor, but it's better. Eric Church's song, 'Wrecking Ball,' began to play through the speakers, and he pulled me closer. I loved this song; apparently, he did, too.

"Ah, Meadow, this song has always made me think of you." He said, stroking the sides of my body, running his hands from my waist up my rib cage and back down again.

I looked up at him in surprise, "really?"

"I always hoped you'd come crashing through my front door," he said with a light chuckle. "Seriously though, I've never stopped thinking about you. I'm scared you're going to leave again." His eyes focused on mine so intently and sincerely that his hands gripped my waist, holding me securely.

My stomach fluttered, and my heart throbbed; the way he looked at me made my legs tremble. I looked back at him; my smile faded as I was deadlocked in his eyes.

"I'm not going anywhere," I said as I slid my hands from his shoulders to the sides of his face, pulling him to me. I couldn't take it anymore. I wanted him, and I needed him. As he followed my lead and lowered his face to mine, I leaned in and kissed him. A slow, gentle kiss on his pouty lips. He backed away, still holding me, but now looking at me confused. Staring at me profoundly as if in a deep thought. Then suddenly, he removed his hands from my body and grabbed my face, drawing me towards him and meeting his lips with me. Kissing me with such passion, lips locked and bodies pressed against each other. His hands moved from my face down my side, further and further. His grasp on my hips slid to my ass, squeezing it and holding me firmly. I raised my arms around his shoulders, holding the back of his head as we continued to kiss. Pressing my breast against his chest and pushing forward my hips to rub against his body. He pulled his lips back from mine and brought them to my neck, pecking gently up and down. I could feel my nipples getting hard. I wanted him so bad. I lusted for him. His lips met mine again as he began to raise the back of my dress up, now rubbing on my bare ass, sliding his fingers through the back of my thong. Teasing me as I became more hot for him. His hands cupped under my ass cheeks tightly as he picked me up and spun me around, sitting me on the tailgate of his truck.

"I want you so bad, Meadow," He said, taking a breath of air from our make-out session. Kissing along my neck, down my collarbone, to the top of my breast. I reached my hands up to the buttons on my dress and began to unbutton them one by one. Revealing my breast, grabbing his hands, and placing them on my chest. He stared into my eyes, rubbing my breast and gently running his fingers across my nipples. Weston leaned forward and kissed me again with such zeal and ardor. It was so hot; he was so hot. His mouth wandered from my lips back to my neck again and then further south. I could feel his breath as his mouth moved to my boobs, softly kissing them. Then his wet tongue emerged and licked my nipple back and forth, one and then the other. Firmly holding my back perched and close as he began to suck on my right tit. Oh my god. I threw my head back and let out a little moan; it felt so good I couldn't contain myself. He moved along my chest, tugging at my nipples with his teeth, licking me, rubbing me, sucking on me gently and then more aggressively. I could feel myself getting wet; I don't think I've ever been so turned on in my life. He then pushed my body back so that I was lying on the flatbed; he stood between my legs. Running his fingers up and down, etching closer to the end of my dress. Slowly rising higher and higher, raising my dress up fully and laying it across my stomach. His hands rubbed across the top of my thong; my legs began to quiver. He lowered his head down, kissing my legs, licking around my panties. His lips moved between my thighs, kissing and biting me. It hurt but felt good, so erotic and desirable. I wanted him more and more. He stood up and grabbed my hands, leading me back to a sitting position.

"Let's get you inside," he said with a grin plastered across his chiseled face. He pulled me up, throwing me over his broad shoulders and smacking my ass. I giggled and kicked my legs as I reached down to hold the back of his belt and keep my buzzed body from falling over. He marched me into the house and up the stairs, kicking open the door to my bedroom and throwing me onto the bed. I laid there, looking up at him between my legs that were bent with my feet firmly planted on the bed. My dress unbutton and breast exposed, nipples hard, waiting for his return. I watched him look me over in the bed, biting his bottom lip. He began to undo his belt and unzip his pants. As he pulled down his Levi's, I could already see the massive bulge poking out from his boxer briefs. My legs quivered more; I needed him on top of me, inside of me. I extended my left leg to tug at the bottom of his underwear with my toes. He tossed his head back and laughed, smacking my foot away in a joking and adorable way. He teased me further by removing his shirt before finally pulling down his boxers. Good lord. His body stood before me like a perfectly sculpted statue. Big and broad, strong and sexy. He came towards me, placing his hands on the bed and then slowly crawling on top of me. Kissing my lips and laying me fully down.

The way he looked in my eyes was as if he could see my soul. So much passion and lust behind them, so intense and yet endearing. Irresistible ultimately. He shifted his mouth once more to my neck, kissing tenderly up and down as he began to slide inside me. I cried out a light gasp as I braced myself for him. I was so tight; it had been over a year since I had sex. Ryan would be too "worked up" or "not in the mood" to make love. I think it was too many pills, and past use of steroids was the actual reason, but I was fine with it anyway. It's hard to get turned on by someone that beats your ass as opposed to smacks it out of lust. Weston buried his head into my neck and moaned as he pushed deeper inside of me. Slow and steady, back and forth, penetrating further. It felt so good I could cry.

"Are you ok?" He whispered in my ear as he nibbled on my lobe and kissed my neck again.

"Yes," I panted as I ran my hands up and down his back, holding him to me. Never wanting him to stop. He started to go harder and faster, again and again. It was incredible and so provocative. Pounding me and moaning, nippling at my neck, he fucking loved it. I loved it. We made love for over an hour that night. Switching positions, biting, licking, groaning, it was so hot and sexy. When we were done, I walked him down the stairs and to the front door.

"Thanks for a great night; I will definitely be adding 'Dinner with Weson' to the menu now that I've experienced it," I laughed as I reached up to kiss him one more time.

"Haha, well, I'm so glad you were pleased with it. I certainly was." He reached down and grabbed my hand, pulling it to his mouth and kissing the top of it. "Goodnight, Meadow; I'll see you tomorrow." He placed his hat on his head, winked at me, and walked out the door. I watched him pull out of the driveway and down the street until he was fully out of my site. I turned around, placing my back against the door, standing there in awe. I grinned to myself, thinking of the night and all that happened. I was still blushing. Weston fucking Ridge, wow. I headed back up the stairs and tucked myself in bed, thinking of my cowboy until I drifted away.

# CHAPTER 12

Waking to the subtle glow sneaking through the slim gaps between my rose patterned curtains; my smile broke just as I rose like the sun. Replaying in my head the actions that took place the night before. I could see the gleam in Weston's eyes across from me, illuminated by the fire between us. I was drawn to him like a moth to a flame. His charm and sex appeal were irresistible. The entire evening was both enchanting and erotic. I could not stop thinking about him, about us. I laid on my pillow top bed, frozen, paralyzed almost, stuck in a trance. Reminiscing about the evening's events, digesting and processing what happened. What had happened. I haven't experienced love like that before. Lust like that before. Pure openness, trust, and freedom with my body like that before. I stretched and giggled softly to myself. I craved to see him again. The thought of him sent goosebumps across my skin and excitement throughout my soul. I couldn't wait to touch him again. Be with him again. Taste him again. I finally managed to crawl out of bed and stagger to the bathroom. Ouch. My entire body ached from our power hour. I was so sore that I could barely sit down on the toilet. When they say pain is pleasure, I could now see why. I slowly stood up from the toilet and edged my way over to start the shower. As the hot water ran and the bathroom filled with steam, I began to undress. Running my hand under the cascading water to test the temperature, I was ready to slip inside. As I slid my pajama shorts off, I noticed something. A bruise. Right on the inside of my thigh, a perfectly 'mouth' shaped bruise. Dark purple and so incredibly tender. Faint teeth marks embedded into my soft skin. Defined and pronounced as a mark left behind during a crime of passion. Resembling an embellished hickey against my ivory complexion, could not be more obvious. Weston. Weston sucked and bit his way up and down my body and left his stamp behind. I grinned and slowly ran my fingers across the mark. For the first time ever, I was happy to have a bruise. Thrilled, in fact.

Work was extremely busy that day, the weather was beautiful, and the rodeo was on that weekend. Vendors, riders, and locals, in anticipation of the big event, were flooding the town streets as well as the cafe. After a long shift, I finally had some downtime in the late afternoon to clean up after the crowds had dissipated. While I was doing some dishes, I heard the front doorbell and peeked around the corner. It was Carol.

"Meadow! Hello darling!" She yelled out, even more chipper than usual.

She was gleaming and heading towards me with a bounce in her step. What got into her? Maybe she and the Mr. had themselves a power hour last night, too.

"Hey, Carol! How are you?"

"Great," she said. "Were you busy today?"

"Yes! Packed, it was great!"

"Good, business is always good. More business, more money," she smirked.

"Yes, ma'am, I agree."

"I do need to talk to you about something if you want to step out here and have a seat, it won't take long," she said.

Oh no, here it is. She must have already found a buyer. That was fast. What will I do now? I love it here. This place is my serenity. I was still nervous about Ryan. In the back of my head, the thought of him hung. Still wanting to stay off the radar was my goal. How could I explain this to someone else? I couldn't just walk into another business, apply for a job, and then demand they pay me in cash so my psychotic husband, who thinks I'm dead, can't find me. I'm not sure that would go over well. I swallowed the lump in my throat and managed to make my way over to the table she was sitting at.

"What's going on, Carol," I asked as I took a chair next to her. She had a manilla folder in front of her and a couple of pens. This was all so odd.

"Well, Meadow. I actually received a phone call this morning from someone interested in purchasing this place."

My heart sank, "Oh really?" I tried to sound excited for her, but my heart instantly started to ache. "For just the building or business as well?"

Carol beamed with excitement, "Both! Yes, Meadow, it was such a surprise to me. Not only do they want to purchase both, but they offered me much more than I was asking for."

"Wow, that's amazing. Good for you, Carol!"

This was good news, great news. Except, well, what if they wanted a new staff? Maybe my job wasn't as secure as I thought it would be.

"Actually, Meadow, it's good for both of us."

Confused, I tilted my head slightly and watched her across the table as she began to open the envelope and pull a stack of papers out.

"How so? Did the new owners say they would keep me on? You know even if they bring a new staff in, they will need someone to train them and someone who is familiar with the locals. Maybe you should tell them that. Just let them know that I'm here and helpful."

She began to laugh and shake her head, "Oh Meadow, you actually will still be very involved." She laid the papers in front of me and sat a pen on top of the pile. "You are the new owner, Meadow."

"Wait, what?!" I gasped as I grabbed the papers and began to scan the documents over.

"Weston Ridge called me this morning asking to meet immediately. He already had a cashier's check ready to go and purchased the building and business at 8 am this morning. He paid for it but wants it in your name. Since it's paid fully in cash, we don't need any loan documents or personal info, just transfer of deed. So, if you would just sign in the marked boxes, it's all yours."

"Oh my god, I can't believe this. I need to call Weston. This is too much. We didn't even discuss this. I'm in shock."

Carol grinned and reached across the table, grabbing my hands and deadlocking on my eyes, "Listen, you've been through a lot and have been handed a new opportunity. Take it. You are happy here. The customers are happy you are here, Weston is happy you are here. Don't push away a good thing, Meadow."

She was right; I was just in shock and surprise, and I didn't really know how to react. Was this really happening? This was unbelievable, surreal.

"Oh my god, Carol, I just can't believe this. Yes, I will sign!" I laughed and grabbed the pen, still in disbelief. "I promise, Carol, I will make you proud and continue to keep this place going as you would."

"I know you will, dear. That's why I'm so excited for this. Excited for you."

We went through the paperwork, simply going over bank accounts and vendors for the business, basic things for the most part. And then, just like that, I signed the papers and became the new owner of Coffee Couture. Carol slid over the keys, gave me a hug, and strutted out the front door. After she left, I held the keys in my hand for so long that my palm began to sweat. Finally, taking a breath, I slowly opened my hand, and there they sat. It was real, this was mine, all mine. I couldn't wait to thank Weston. This was the most amazing thing anyone had ever done for me. Most guys send flowers, but not this man, though. He's not that simple. He's a cowboy. Cowboys do big things. My heart was full, so full it felt as if it could burst. I finished my shift, cleaned up, and locked the doors. I was ready to find my rancher and celebrate.

I hopped in my car and headed towards the field. I knew Weston was farming. It was about 10 minutes from the shop on my way home. Perfect pit stop. As I drove to him, I began to think how lucky I was. Everything I had expected for life to be didn't exist. I had spent the last 6 years of my life in misery and fear. I wish I had left sooner. I had been missing out on so much. THIS is what it means to be living.

Home with my mom, a job that I love, a man who adores me. It didn't matter anymore what my expectations were or whether I had failed or succeeded at this point. I only had the future to look forward, and my eyes were set straight ahead.

I pulled onto the side road of the field, where I could see Weston in the distance on the combine. I honked and waved my hand out the window to get his attention. Weston had been a farm manager for the past 4 years, but he still maintained his dad's business as well, Ridge Family Farms, with his two brothers, Tanner and Evan. He waved back and headed my way. It was a beautiful day; the sky was crystal clear, and there was not a cloud in sight. The contrast from the periwinkle backdrop cascading across acres of ebony, soiled ground made for a lovely canvas.

"Hello, ma'am," Weston smirked as he opened his door, turned off the engine, and tipped his cowboy hat my way. "Need a ride?" he grinned and tapped his hands on his lap.

I laughed, "No, I don't need a ride. Just wanted to chat."

"I see, what about Miss Meadow?"

"You know exactly what!" I placed my hands on my hips and raised my eyebrows to him as a smile stretched across my face. "I heard you had a meeting with Carol this morning?"

"Ah ha, yes, I did. Congrats on the new gig."

"Stop it! Weston, you are too much!" I laughed and ran over to him, climbing up to him, one foot on the step, and then pulling myself into the cab. I threw my arms around his neck and leaned into him. "Thank you, thank you so much." I pulled him close to me by the back of his neck and kissed him.

"You are very welcome. You said it makes you happy. I want you to stay happy."

"You are so sweet. It's just too much, though. I want to pay you back over time. I don't want to feel like I owe you."

He chuckled, "Owe me? I bought it for YOU, it's yours. Bottom line plain and simple. But...if you feel the need to pay me back, I do enjoy small favors."

"Really," I said, grinning and kissing on his neck. Pecking gently up and down, nibbling every so slightly on his ear lobe.

"Oh yes, why don't you just climb all the way in here and take a seat so I can shut this door." He grabbed me firmly by the hips, leaned up, and kissed me hard and passionately. He spun my body around so that my ass was placed on his lap, my back to him. He whispered in my ear, "Shut the door, please."

I reached over and pulled the door closed as he began to kiss my neck and run his hands up and down my legs. His right hand edged higher up my thigh now, sliding his fingers back and forth under the base of my terry cloth shorts, teasing me with his soft touch. His left hand slowly began to shift up my leg, then my torso, and then my breast. Squeezing and rubbing my left breast and then rolling over to my other, moving his hand down the top of my shirt and playing with my nipples.

It felt so good. He turned me on so much. I began to move my hips back and forth, circling his hard-on and pressing against it. He grabbed my right leg and pulled it back to where my foot was no longer flat, and my knee was bent. Bringing his hand back to the inside of my leg, running his fingers up my shorts, and sliding my thong to the side. His index finger stroked the inside of me, gently rubbing on my lips and then inside of me. I moved more and turned my head back to kiss him. I wanted more, but I couldn't take it. He brought his finger up to my mouth and slid it in delicately. I licked it and sucked on it, getting it wet. Bringing his hand back down, he pushed his finger inside of me. Slow and easy at first, in and out. His other hand was still holding my panties to the side as he thrust his finger harder and deeper inside of me. I looked down and watched as he did it. It was so hot. He fingered me until I came. I was so wet he removed his finger and pushed my ass up. Lifting me off of him, leaning me over the steering wheel. He unfastened his belt, lowered his zipper, and slid his jeans off. He grabbed me by the waist and pulled down on him hard. It took my breath away. He pushed inside of me, moving my hips back and forth towards him. I howled. He was so deep. It hurt. I was already sore from the night before. But I liked it. I didn't want him to stop.  His hands raced across my chest, rubbing my breast, pinching and pulling at my nipples. It was so provocative, so dirty. I never had a passion like this. Lusted for someone like this. He was so aggressive, and I loved it. I had never had such pain that I desired. It was so ironic as, not too long ago, I left someone for hurting me. Now, I ran to someone for pain, pleasurable pain. I loved it.

When he finished, he helped me out of the combine and walked me to my car. Holding my hand and then smacking my ass as he approached my car door. He spun me around and pulled me down on him, hard.

"Thank you for that lovely afternoon delight," he grinned widely and then kissed my nose and then my lips. "See you tonight for dinner. Tell Mama I'm bringing her Chinese food again."

He winked at me and walked away. Hauling himself up into the machinery and riding off into the sunset. My wild western would make for a good dirty novel.

# CHAPTER 13

It had been well over a month since I ran out of my Chicago suburban life to save my own. Leaving no trace of me behind, faking my own death, and finally escaping the torturous grasp of Ryan Cooper. Or, at least, I thought I had.

While I was busy starting over where I started from, my past was not as far behind me as I thought. Ryan had been a miserable wreck, lost and in despair since my death. Feeling remorse and guilt for his actions, and how he treated me. Blaming himself for my tragic accident and untimely death. Weeks passed, and he had finally decided to sell our home and move into a condo overlooking the city. As Ryan was packing things up gradually, he came across a filing cabinet in our home office. He brought out a box and placed it on the oak desk that sat near the cabinet to place the fillings inside. At first, he began grabbing handfuls of papers and setting them on top of each other in the box. After a couple of times, some papers slipped from his grasp and fell to the floor. Ryan leaned down to pick them up and came across a paper with the heading, 'Hummingbird Homes Assisted Living Facility, Lexington, Kentucky.'

Confused, he brought the paper closer to his face, studying the document closely. Thinking to himself, what is this? Where did this come from? When was this? He thought to himself how my mom had passed. Was she placed in a home prior to that? He then began to feel bad once again, as he could admit to himself that he truly never paid attention to what I said. How bad of a husband he was and how he wished he could have been better. He dismissed the paper and placed it aside as he continued to pack the remaining papers up. After a few more minutes, he came to a halt once again. Another document with the same heading, but this wasn't a general information letter. This was a residence agreement letter. Not only a residence agreement letter, but also an attached invoice which showed a payment made 6 months ago.

Ryan's eyes widened. He read through the paper over and over. Bewildered at what he was seeing. Thinking to himself, why would payments be made to a home where someone had passed? He couldn't let the thought go. He rummaged through the rest of the materials, searching for any other relatable content. Nothing, not a trace. Just these 2 papers. They were enough, though, to spark his curiosity. He decided to call the number listed on the sheet for Hummingbird Homes.

"Thank you for calling Hummingbird Homes. This is Renee. How can I assist you today?"

Ryan cleared his throat, "Hello, yes, I came across an invoice and believe there's been a mistake. You see, my mother-in-law passed away a couple of years ago, and I think you have been charging my wife accidentally still."

"Oh sir, well, let's look into this. Could you give me your mother-in-law's name, and I can see what I can find? I'm very sorry for your loss as well," she said empathetically.

"Thank you, I appreciate that. Her name was Jennifer Williams, I believe, but am not sure that my wife had placed her there after her dad passed. But as I said, her mother passed away a couple years ago from a stroke, so there must be some mistake."

"When was the invoice you saw sir, how long ago?" Renee asked, her voice becoming confused and unsteady now.

"I just came across one. It was dated 6 months ago."

"Hmmm, well this is odd. You say she passed away a couple of years ago, but she was still here just until last month."

Ryan's temple began to throb. He was baffled, angry, in shock. His mind began to race. He was overwhelmed with panic and confusion, "Wait, what? What are you saying? How could she be there until last month if she died years ago? This doesn't make any sense."

"I'm so sorry sir. I'm not sure myself what is going on, but I can tell you she is alive and well, at least since last month."

He became more furious and baffled, "You keep saying last month, what happened to her last month?"

"Well, her daughter came and checked her out, sir."

"Her daughter? My wife was an only child and passed away recently. Who picked her up?"

"Oh no, sir, I'm so sorry! Umm, let me look here. On the release forms, it says Meadow Williams. Is that another relative, sir? Sir, are you still there, sir....?"

All Renee heard from that point on was the dial tone. Ryan hung up, gripping his phone close to his chest, pacing the room like a caged tiger. He threw his phone across the room and screamed with rage. He marched back to the box on the desk that had been filled with the findings from the filing cabinet. Ryan grabbed the box and dumped the papers all over the floor. Dropping his body to his knees, shuffling through each document. Examining closely, looking for any other clues or information. Thinking to himself, what is going on? This can't be real. She's dead. She died. Or did she? Why did she tell me her mom had passed if she didn't? Is someone else using Meadow's name? None of this made sense to him. He felt out of control and frustrated. He went ballistic. Riffling through every closet, cabinet, and drawer. Searching for an answer. Nothing.

He waltzed over to the bar in the dining area and took a deep breath as he poured himself a shot of Johnny Walker Blue Label and scanned the room. His eyes ran across the home as he walked every foot of the house. Thinking to himself, there has to be something here. There has to be something left behind, a sign of some sort. Did she fake her own death to escape me? Is she really still alive? Where is she, where is SHE? He made his way back to the bar and poured another shot, throwing it back and filling his cup once more. Thinking to himself, searching his mind, replaying the night in his head where I dashed out the door. For weeks, no sign of me. No inkling that I might still, somehow, be alive until now. No phone record, no bank activity, nothing. Wait, he thought, bank activity. He slammed his glass down and ran down the hall, snatching the invoice off of the desk. He moved his eyes down the sheet until he came across the billing section. The last 4 numbers of the credit card used for payment were listed. All of our cards were linked and matched. He reached into his back pocket, retrieving his wallet. Yanking out all of his debit and credit cards, looking over the numbers for a match. Nothing matched.

In frustration, he took a seat in the chair facing the desk and turned on the computer. He logged into our bank account and began searching the transaction history. He scrolled for what felt like forever, looking for anything unusual. After a few minutes, there it was: a withdrawal of $500 from 5 weeks ago. And another one the week prior, and another one the week before that, and so on for 9 months. $18,000 in withdrawals total that he never knew of because he never looked. I handled all the bills and finances; my plan to run was right under his unsuspecting nose, and he was enraged.

"Meadow!!!" He screamed from behind his desk. "You fucking bitch!"

He stood up and slammed his fist down, smashing the computer. Pushing everything off the desk and kicking the chair across the room. His heart raced, his eyes bulged, his face red, and his chest raised. He was in a fit of rage when he spotted his phone across the room that he had thrown earlier. He ran over to grab it and began to dial the number to his office.

"Hey, this is Ryan. I need you to book me a flight. Lexington, Kentucky, the earliest flight they have available tomorrow. Email me the details immediately."

He hung up his phone and walked into the bedroom to pack a bag. As he rummaged through his drawers, snatching clothes and throwing them into his suitcase, he slammed the drawer too hard and knocked over our wedding photo that was sitting on top of the furniture. He stared at the photo at first, laying flat on top of the solid oak space. He slowly reached over to the framed photo and picked it up. Running his hand along the picture, circling my face with his finger tips.

"Til death do us part, my dear," he whispered before throwing the picture at the wall, shattering the glass into tiny pieces.

Ryan took the first flight out of O'Hare to Lexington at 7:10 am that next morning. Landing in the southern city and renting a car from the airport. He tossed his bag in the trunk, started the engine, and typed into the navigation, 'Hummingbird Homes.' As he pulled up to the facility, he shut off the car and thought for a moment about his approach. He wanted to walk calmly and charmingly. He couldn't let them see him concerned or confused. He needed information. He was used to flashing his smile and having women fall at their feet to him. However, he did worry about Renee, who he spoke to the day prior, being at the front desk. This wouldn't work if she was there. Ryan then reached for his phone and called the front desk.

"Thank you for calling Hummingbird Homes. This is Tammy, how can I help you?"

Click. He ended the call and once again placed the phone near his chest, but this time not enraged. This time smiling, almost laughing to himself. He glanced up in the mirror, checking his reflection, slicked his hair back, and grinned once more. Stepping out of the car, he strutted into Hummingbird Homes like a smooth criminal. As he approached the front desk, he noticed he had already caught Tammy's attention, as she was staring in dismay. Ryan may be a psycho, but he is handsome when he doesn't have a scowl on his face or isn't chasing you around the house with a golf club. He was a city businessman, distinguished and well-mannered. He knew how to flatter women and flash money. He was a different breed than those in Kentucky, which naturally caught the eye of Miss Tammy working the front desk.

"Hello sir, how can I help you today?" she cheerfully asked as she blushed and grinned at Ryan.

Ryan leaned in, placing his palms on the desktop and lowering his head down towards her. Making her blush even more as he was looking into her eyes and moving closer.

"Well, ma'am, it's actually kind of embarrassing," he grinned and chuckled, shrugging his shoulders slightly. "My wife actually just took her mother out of here, and I'm in town from Chicago and came to surprise them for a visit. But...I messed up, I forgot the address, and I've been trying to call my wife but the cell service isn't the best out in the country. I just get confused around this area and need a little direction, if you could be so sweet to help me?"

He sounded sincere and genuine. She couldn't resist the pitifulness of his voice or the endearing look in his eyes.

"Awww sugar, that is so nice of you to surprise them. They will love that!"

"Thank you. I have a couple of bouquets of flowers in the car, too. I'm ready," he laughed and winked across the desk at the lady.

"Well, let me see what I can do to help. What's the name, sir?"

"It's Jennifer Williams. My wife just got her last month but it's my first time being back here in years. Did she leave a forwarding address, perhaps?"

"Hmm, let me pull it up and see," Tammy entered a few things on the keyboard and then began to scroll through. "Yep, here it is! Let me write this down for you, honey." She grabbed a yellow post-it and pen and jotted down the address. Ripping it from the pad of paper, she handed it across the desk to Ryan. "There you go, dear. Good luck with the surprise!"

He took the paper and studied it before folding it in half and sliding it into his pocket. His face lit up as he beamed back at her, "Thank you very much. It will be a great surprise indeed."

Ryan jumped in the car and headed to Versailles, a 25-minute drive to me. To find me. To kill me.

He cruised the town streets, making his way to my childhood home. My sanctuary, my safe place. His black Lexus rental car patrolled the area, creeping closer to my house. As he approached the fence line to my property, he stared and stretched his head as far out of the window as he could. Examining the property thoroughly, just as I did only a few short weeks earlier upon my return. He pulled into the driveway, studying the place. He took out his cell phone, took some pics of the house, and then slowly backed the car out and left. Ryan made his way through town and checked into a little Bed and Breakfast in the area. Settling into his room and ordering delivery from the nearby wood-fired pizza joint, he brought out a laptop from his bag. Pulling up Google, he typed, 'Jennifer and Larry Williams Versailles, Kentucky.' There populated articles of my parents and their furniture store, "bingo," he said as his eyes widened and his smile broadened.

Once he finished his pizza and showered, he took off again. This time in search of my parents' furniture store, Williams West Designs.

My father's name, obviously, was Williams, but my mother's maiden name was West. That's where they came up with the name for the business. As his car pulled into the location where my parents prized possession once stood, all he saw was a vacant lot and an abandoned building. Once, a bustling business known not just by the locals but by people who would travel from miles away just for my dad's custom craftsmanship was gone. Ryan emerged from the vehicle and walked along the sides of the building, cupping his hands around his eyes and looking in through the windows. Standing back, looking at the building, he walked by the car in defeat.

"I'll find you soon, honey," he whispered to himself as he pulled out of the parking lot and went back to his room for the evening.

By 6 am the next morning, Ryan was parked outside of my house. Down the street and back into the tree line, where he wasn't visible to me, but I was directly in his sight. Parked precisely enough out of vision but focused on my front door. Following me to my work, my shop, my new business. He crept behind me at a distance, not drawing any attention to himself. I whipped into my usual parking spot outside of the cafe, about five spots down from the front door. I never parked directly in front of the shop. I always saved those front-row spaces for guests. As I unlocked the front door to my cafe and entered the building, Ryan watched from his car across the street. He was captivated and couldn't believe what he was seeing with his own eyes. Finding documentation, speaking with the receptionist, and hearing that I'm alive was far different than witnessing it with his own two eyes. Stunned and shocked, his blood began to boil as he felt like a fool. He mourned the loss of me for weeks, blamed himself, cried and wept, and all for nothing. I was alive. I was alive and well.

An evil smile lurked across his face as he gazed in my direction, snarling to himself, "Found you."

# CHAPTER 14

Work was busy, even busier than the day prior, and more riders and vendors were coming into town as we got closer to the weekend and the rodeo. It was so fun having the random visitors in the cafe. This rodeo brought in people from all over the country in all shapes and sizes and different accents too. I also was learning to do the inventory, ordering, books, and other "business owner" tasks as the day went on. Life was good; I was happy. There was truly nothing else I could ask for. Then, Weston walked into the cafe carrying a puppy. Well, I guess there is ONE more thing I could ask for.

"Oh my god!! Who is this Weston?" I cried out as I ran over to him, reaching out and grabbing the puppy from his arms. I picked him up and held him close to me; he snuggled his little furry face under my chin and wagged his tail.

"Well, he doesn't have a name yet, but I thought I'd leave that to you. But I was thinking, your mom needs a companion. I thought he'd be good for her, you know?"

Ugh, this man. I held the puppy securely with one hand and reached my other one around Weston, pulling my body into him. "You are the sweetest man I've ever met," I gushed as I looked deep into his eyes and planted a big, fat kiss on his pouty, soft lips. "What should we name him?" I turned the puppy on his back, cradling him like a baby so I could get a good look at his face. He was a yellow lab, but not so much yellow; he was more beige with sandy brown eyes.

Absolutely adorable; my heart melted. "Let's call him Shadow; he will be Mama's little shadow, follow her everywhere, and keep her company."

"Perfect, Meadow, I love it," he said as he stretched his arms out to grab the pup back. "I'll stop and get a dog bed and puppy chow and then take him to your house. I'll see you when you close up." He took the pooch, gave me a smooch, and headed out the door. A couple of hours had passed, and it was closing time. I was beaten, my feet and back were sore, and I was exhausted. I was more than ready to get home to my sweet pup and sweetheart. I couldn't wait to see mama's reaction to Shadow; she is going to be thrilled. It is exactly what she needs: a little friend to keep her busy and someone to care for. I always tried to keep her mind and body in motion, just trying to fight off the progression of the dementia for as long as possible. I have read before that pets are great for dementia and Alzheimer's patience. But, in all seriousness, who are pets not great for? Man's best friend, right?

I flicked off the lights, threw my purse over my shoulder, and headed out the door. As I began to walk to my car, I noticed something on my windshield. What was it? It was kind of hard to make out at first; all I could really tell was that it was red. As I approached the side of my vehicle, I could now clearly see the image. It was a red rose. A single red rose, so vibrant and vividly bright, and beautiful. Ahh Weston. It's never enough with him, a puppy and a rose? This guy is golden. I was falling harder by the day for this cowboy. Lockstruck, I grabbed the flower from the car and hopped in. I cruised home with the windows down and wind in my hair, not a care in the world. Just a feeling of bliss, total and complete bliss, that I never wanted to end.

After supper, Weston and I took mama and Shadow for a walk around the property. It was great watching my mom with the puppy. She was in love! Shadow would run along beside us, ears flapping so hard I thought he was going to take off flying at any time. He was the cutest thing; it was adorable watching him pounce around the yard chasing butterflies. Mom laughed and laughed, watching him squirm around in the grass, poking his tilted head up with one ear flopped over. He was wild but also a little snuggler. You could pick him up and hold him like a baby, and he'd just look over your shoulder, perfectly content. He completely occupied moms time and filled her heart. What a great idea. Weston Ridge strikes again. As my mom took a seat on the old, rusty iron bench that sat beside the pond, I made my way over to Weston. His silhouette against the sunset, with the reflection of the day's late rays cascading over the pond, was beautiful. He was beautiful, but just not physically, internally. His soul was as good as gold, and his heart was pure; he was one of a kind.

"Thank you for this; thank you for everything," I whispered to Weston as I stepped into him, wrapping my arms around his body. I held him so tight and buried my head in his chest. He leaned his chin down on to the top of my head and placed both hands on my back, holding me closer.

"You're welcome, baby." He spoke softly into my ear before kissing my cheek and down my neck until I began to giggle uncontrollably and had to break free from his grasp.

"Get out of there!" I laughed as I swatted at him. "Oh god, I almost forgot! Thanks also for the gorgeous rose; you really are too good for me." I lunged back at him, squeezing him tight once more. However, he didn't embrace me with the same enthusiasm as last time.

"What flower, babe?" He said, confused.

I stepped back from him so that I could look at his face. Was he messing with me? I giggled, "Come on, stop. The red rose? The red rose you put on my windshield today?"

"I'm not joking, swear!" He held up his hands and crossed his fingers, scouts honor style.

"Really?" Now, I was confused.

"Yeah, really, that's weird. Was there a note or anything else?"

"No, just the rose tucked into the windshield wiper."

Weston rubbed his hand across his chin, "looks like someone has a secret admirer!" He chuckled as he tickled me.

"Stop it, oh my god, that's ridiculous! Someone probably mistook my car for someone else's, is all."

He shook his head and smirked, "Naw, I bet it's one of the old man ranchers that come in the mornings for their coffee and war stories."

We both burst out with laughter and headed back over to mom and Shadow. It was getting late, and I wanted to get her inside and clean up the kitchen before bed. I knew Weston had an early day, too. He was an exhibitor for the upcoming rodeo, so he needed to be at the site around 6 am to oversee the set up of their display and arena. I helped mom change into her nightgown. She struggles with her shoulder after the stroke sometimes and settles into bed. I headed back into the kitchen, where Weston was doing the dishes. Mr. America's Sweetheart over here. I crept up behind him on my tip toes until I landed directly behind him. I slid my hands around his waist and up to his chest. Then, slowly towards me again, caressing his back and rubbing his shoulders.

"Now this," he said with his dimples popping, "is what I consider a fair trade." I laughed and hugged him, laying my head on his broad back. This was nice. I backed away from him and started to walk over to Shadow's kennel. Weston had bought a little doggy bed earlier, and I wanted to place it inside and give our new little baby a nice cushion to crash on. As I reached down for the dog bed, the phone rang. The house phone, the old landline we've had for roughly 30 years. I know they're a rare commodity these days, but we believe in vintage goods around here. That's actually a lie; I could care less about early-century technology. However,  my mother wouldn't know what to do with a cell phone, so I like the land line in case there's an emergency, and she can at least dial 9-1-1 (fingers crossed anyway).

Reaching to answer the phone, I looked over at Weston and shrugged my shoulders. "Hello?" Nothing, I mean something, it wasn't dead air, I could hear breathing. Very heavy breathing but nothing more. Maybe they didn't hear me, probably one of my mom's older friends. So, I repeated myself, "Hello?" Again, just breathing surrounded by silence. My eyes wandered over to Weston, who was now done doing the dishes and leaning his back against the sink, watching me. "Hello? Hello? Anyone there?"

Click. They hung up. I placed the phone back on the hook and stood there still for a moment, staring at the phone. Something didn't feel right. It didn't feel like a standard prank phone call. It wasn't dead air or static; it was someone calling just to listen. It was eerie and odd; the hairs on the back of my neck began to rise, and goosebumps bubbled up along my arms. I shivered and crossed my arms around my body, looking across the room at Weston. "Prank phone call, I guess." I walked away from the phone and headed back to the dog bed.

"What did they say, Meadow?"

"Nothing, they didn't say anything. But someone was there; I could hear them breathing. It was weird. Like I said, it's just kids playing around, probably."

Weston could tell I was shaken and uncomfortable, but I didn't know why I couldn't brush it off. I couldn't shake the feeling that something seemed wrong; it shouldn't have been that big of a deal, but something wasn't settling right. "Hey babe, are you sure they didn't say anything else? I want you to tell me, ok?" He wrapped his arms around my waist and kissed me on my forehead.

"Oh no, I swear that's all it was. I just, I don't know, something just struck me. It's the way they were breathing. It was so heavy and intense. Like, someone with a bunch of adrenaline running, does that make sense? Very hard, fast-paced, aggressive breathing. It was just strange."

His eyebrows lowered, he began to frown, and his sweet smile became stern and serious. "Hey, look at me, Meadow," he grabbed my chin, pushing it up until we were locking eyes. "Hey, you HAVE to tell me if you get any other calls. I don't like this. It really makes me more curious about that rose you got on your car today. I'm going to call Tanner and have him meet Evan to set up tomorrow; I'm going to go to work with you."

"Oh, Weston, no! It's not that serious; it could just be a random coincidence. I'll be fine; you can call and check on me anytime."

"Are you sure? It's really no problem, and I'd be more comfortable with that."

I began to laugh and started to push him towards the door, "it's time for bed, Mister; you have a very long day tomorrow."

"Are you kicking me out, Meadow Williams?" He stumbled back as I scooted him closer to the door, chuckling and raising his hands up in the air. "Ok, ok, I give up. You win; I'm leaving and going home. You have a good night, babe; I will see you tomorrow." He planted a kiss on my lips and headed out the door.``

I waved to him from the front porch and blew him a kiss, "bye, cowboy!"

He yelled at me as he stepped into his truck, "Get in and lock the doors now! Please." He chuckled, blew me a kiss back, and drove off.

I went back inside and immediately locked all the windows and doors. I know I was probably overthinking it but that call, I couldn't get it out of my head. After closing up the homestead with my security patrol walk, I went back to set up Shadow. I loaded his kennel up with his dog bed and pee pad and baited the little love bug in with a treat. Then I took a much-needed long, hot shower and lathered myself up with moisturizer before slipping into my satin pajamas and fuzzy slippers. Ahh, the best feeling. That freshly bathed, shaved, and silky feeling you get after an overdue shower. It's the little things in life. As I was patting my damp hair with a towel, I walked across my bedroom, turned off my lap, and settled in bed. I tossed the towel down on my chair near my bed and bent over to shut off the light. When I stood back up to close the curtains, I saw something through the window. A light. Lights actually. Were those headlights? Looming in the distance, deep at the edge of my driveway facing my house. I instantly ducked down, below the window pain. I was on the second floor, and the room was dark; I don't think they could see me. But did they see me already? Were they watching me that whole time, just now?

My heart began to race, and I had goosebumps again. It was hard to breathe, and I felt like I was suffocating. I sat still, silent. Trying to catch my breath, I closed my eyes and inhaled deeply, then exhaled slowly. I shifted my body so that I could face the wall right below the window. Squatted in the corner of the window, I carefully raised my head a little at a time, just enough so my eyes could peek over and look out the window. It was still there, engine running, headlights on, no music, no person. Shit, my phone was still in the bathroom. I was scared to try to grab it and risk whoever was out there from seeing me. The hall light was on, and there was no way I'd be able to walk by without being visible. What should I do? Who is this? Why are all of these things happening tonight?

I pivoted my body to try to adjust my view once more. I needed to at least see the make and model or the plates, anything that I could at least report later. That's it, I suddenly remembered something. There was a small hutch I was crouched next to that sat against the wall in my room. It's been there ever since I can remember. I can't imagine all the random and crazy things that are probably in there. I'm guessing I could rifle through it and stumble across a Rubix cube, maybe a jump rope, tea set, barbie, or two for sure, but that's not what I needed from there right now. It was the binoculars. I opened the cabinet door and quietly moved my hands around, feeling in the dark for my peekers. Boom! There they were. I can't believe I remembered those were in there. I used to watch my horses out of my window when I was little; I would whisper goodnight to them all before saying my prayers and going to bed.

I shuffled my body back over below the window and perched myself in position as I brought the binoculars to my eyes. They're leaving! Thank god, there they go, backing out of the driveway. I leaned in, focusing to see clearly and still trying to get some visual. It was black, I think a Lexus. It was hard to see as they were going further away from me, but I'm pretty sure that's the Lexus logo. It was sleek and sharp and sat lower to the ground. You don't see a lot of luxury sedans or sports cars in this area. This is the land of big trucks and SUVs, where wealth meets practicality. It's a farm community; many wives work with their husbands, manage their business, and often pick supplies for them or deliver lunch out to the field. Don't get me wrong, there is money in this town, lots of money. I'm not saying people aren't driving Lexus and Cadillacs around here, just not small sedans.

This didn't make sense, none of it. Was the person in the car the same as the one who called? "What rose, babe?" He asked bewildered. It is the same person also, right? It had to be; this is all too ironic. Who would do this? Who would want to frighten me and give me a flower? It just doesn't add up. Or does it? My eyes began to well up and then flooded with tears before I knew it. It does add up. It all adds up. Why am I naive and blind? Ryan, it has to be Ryan. I slid to the ground, falling over and laying flat on the floor. I stared at the ceiling and followed the groves and ridges along the trim. Crying, holding my hands together across my chest, I began to shiver. I felt sick, incredibly sick, and faint. I ran to the bathroom as I was pulling my hair back into a ponytail; I barely made it to the edge of the toilet before I threw up. Body jolting sickness. It felt as if my soul had been torn out of me, and my vessel was crashing. I wanted to sink into the floor. Unsteady on my legs, I held the banister and slowly crept down the stairs. I lightly threaded across the house and slipped into bed with Mama. I was too scared to sleep alone. I was too scared to sleep at all.

# CHAPTER 15

The next day, Weston met me at the cafe during my shift, and I told him about the mystery car that had arrived after he had left.

"Meadow, do you really think it's Ryan? You said he doesn't know you lived here or even that your mom's still alive." He leaned over the counter and looked around to see if anyone was in hearing range as he whispered to me," You crashed the car, blew it up even. Why would he have any reason to believe you are still alive? Or that you are here? I think it's some creep that sees you here and follows you home. There's no way it would be him. And if it was, would he stalk you like this? He sounds controlling and insane, the type of person that wouldn't wait but would just attack."

Pondering his words, I began to think of what had all happened and that he was right. I planned my escape for months, waiting for the right time to leave. I diligently monitored my transactions, mail, and even phone calls to Mama. If he thought I was dead, why would he come to look for me? How would he know to look for me here? I was overreacting and needed to calm down. It was over; it was all over.

"Yeah, that's true. I need to relax, you're right. There's no reason he would come looking for me."

"I understand completely, babe. You are getting scared. Why? I really don't think it could be him. I mean, let's really think about what happened the last couple of days. "First, you find a rose on your car.

That could be from a customer or even put on the wrong car; nothing threatening or scary, though. The phone call could have just been some old man who got confused and called the wrong number, "Or maybe someone placed the flower on the wrong car". And the car, maybe that was someone lost, and they just sat there until they got their navigation straight and then left. You know how confusing it can be in the country for people visiting the area. It is the week of the rodeo, ya know?"

I smiled and rubbed his hands, "Thanks for making me feel better, babe."

"That's what I'm here for," he grinned and kissed me. "I gotta go back to the rodeo and check on the guys, pick you up at 6?"

"Yes! I can't wait, see you then!" It was the first day of the rodeo, and we were going to watch the barrel races that evening. I powered through an incredibly busy shift, anticipating my evening with Weston. It took me over an hour to clean up after closing due to the extra traffic from the weekend event in town. As I grabbed my things and walked to the front door to leave, I stopped dead in my tracks. A black Lexus sedan began to roll slowly through the town street and past my store windows. I could suddenly hear the beating of my heart as my breath became shallow, watching the car. I don't think I blinked as I stood in fear, watching the car pull into a parking spot beside mine. Steadily and slowly, I reached back up and turned the knob to lock the front door of the cafe. Tucking my body behind the wooden paneling, I kept my focus on the Lexus. After parking, the car sat for a few seconds before shutting the engine off. The windows were tinted. I couldn't even make out a shadow of an image in the vehicle. Finally, the driver's door opened, but no one appeared yet. I couldn't breathe; I felt sick again. After waiting and watching, after a few seconds, there was finally movement. Wait, the passenger door is opening now, too. There are two people stalking me? Oh my god. I am an idiot. Two old ladies emerged from the car with their organza derby tea hats and Birkin bags. I exhaled and started to laugh. I was relieved and ridiculous. I giggled once more and rolled my eyes at myself. The ladies stepped out of the car and headed to the boutique next door. Paranoia got the best of me; it was time to unwind with Weston and shrug off this feeling once and for all.

After cooking dinner for Mom and taking Shadow out for a walk, I hopped in the shower and began to shuffle through my closet. I hadn't gone shopping for clothes since I'd been back home. I had limited availability, and I was seeing what I could still squeeze into at this point. Sliding the hangers back and forth, I narrowed down a selection between a couple of sundresses that looked like good prospects. After trying them on and being criticized by my own mirror, I ended with a periwinkle baby doll dress. The material was a little stretchy, so it wrapped around the curves of my breast tightly, showing immense cleavage. It fit   snugly at the waist and then flared out slightly before my knees. It was cool and comfortable, perfect for a stuffy and humid night at the rodeo. I paired the dress with my cowboy boots and tossed my hair up in a messy bun. I lined my lips and lubed them with a shimmering rose pink gloss, dusted some bronzer on my cheeks, and ran down the stairs just as my cowboy was coming up the driveway.

The rodeo was packed and thriving. People everywhere and of all ages swarmed the fairground. The aroma of funnel cakes and turkey legs saturated the air, streaming from the massive line of food trucks. The petting zoo was full of goats and sheep, nibbling food from the tiny hands of the adoring children inside. The laughter of the kids was adorable and infectious, and I instantly giggled while watching them as we passed by. We headed over to the vendor exhibit for Ridge Family Farms and chatted with Tanner and Evan before taking out seats in the grandstand for the steer roping. I hadn't been to one of these events in years since high school, I suppose. I forgot how fun it truly was. The energy in the atmosphere, the entertainment, the food, the animals, the people, it was everything I missed. I really am a country girl at heart; this is where I belong and always have.

As the competition came to an end, Weston wrapped his arm around me and pulled me close. He turned to me and, pecked my neck gently, and lightly breathed against my ear. I could feel the hair on my arms stand up. His hand slid up my leg, flirting with the edge of my dress. Very quietly, he asked, "wanna go for a walk?" A grin shot across my face as I nodded and reached down, grabbing his hand from my leg. "Let's go." He said as he gripped my hand and slid his fingers in between mine, leading me down from the bleachers. We wandered throughout the fairgrounds towards the horse trailers in the back lot. The barrel races were about to begin, so this area was pretty quiet and cleared out. All of the activities and commotion were behind us as we slipped into the shadows out of sight. Weston pulled my hand, gesturing for me to walk in front of him between two livestock trucks. Nestled in the narrow space with just a dim glow from the moon shining onto us, Weston pushed me back against the trailer and began to kiss me. Running his hands up and down my body, he pressed against my breast. Rubbing and squeezing them, sliding his hands up my chest and to my shoulders. Gently lifting the straps to my dress and then yanking them down until my boobs were out. He bent down, lowering himself to face my chest. Grabbing both breasts and pushing them together, licking one and then over the other. Teasing my hard nipples with nibbles and bites, tugs that hurt just enough to feel good. So good.

He stood all the way up and grabbed the sides of my arms, spinning me around like a top. He pressed me up against the trailer and lifted the back of my dress, holding my back firmly with one hand; he smacked my ass cheek with the other. Again and then again, harder, it lifted my heels off the ground. I could hear him breathe louder and more rapidly; he was so intense and passionate. His hands spread across both cheeks, clenching them with his strong grip. Rising up further until he reached the top of my thong, slipping his fingers softly between the stringy material and my skin. Sliding across to the sides where my panties rested on my hips. Tugging them down while stretching them wide enough until they ripped apart and fell to my feet. Leaning into me, pressing his body against my back, he whispered in my ear, "I guess you won't need these anymore."

I giggled and reached my hand back, feeling for his hard-on through his jeans. He pushed my hand down, "Not yet," he smirked. Squatting down behind me, he shoved my legs apart and crawled his fingers up my thigh. Sliding his fingertips gently between my legs until he was taunting my clit, stroking so softly, arousing me indefinitely. I could feel his hand slip away from inside of me, and then nothing. I stood there hot ass out, excited, anxious, waiting, patiently waiting for his next move. Suddenly, his wet tongue ran across my lips, inserting itself inside of me. Back and forth he licked, at first so softly and slow, then with more pressure and faster. This must be why they say, "Eating me out," he acted so hungry. Like a caged, starving animal.  He didn't miss a spot, either. His tongue traced my labia as if it were a map, leading him to a pot of gold. Pushing his head further in between my legs, forcing my knees to straighten, I arched my back and popped my ass up more. Giving him more space as he nudged further, reaching my clit. His deep strokes of the tongue that first found me were now sharp, aggressive flicks onto my clit. Oh my god. It felt so good I started to move my hips across his mouth, riding his face. His hands shot up the sides of my legs, holding me tight, tongue sharp and wet. Bouncing it on me over and over until I came. I cried out and laid my head against the trailer; my legs trembled as I whimpered and tried to catch my breath. My heart was pounding, and my toes curled within my leather boots.

He rose up behind me, wrapping his arms around me and holding me close to him. Ever so quietly, he said, "That was so hot Meadow." He grazed my ear with his lips and took a hard nibble at my neck. I groaned again. "You really turned me on, baby." He whispered as he dropped his jeans to the floor. "Put your hands out in front of you, babe; bend over for me." I stretched my arms out before me, placing my palms firmly against the trailer. He reached down, spreading my legs further apart with his hands, adjusting my body, and repositioning my dress so it rested on my lower back. Snatching my hips, he held tight as he shoved himself inside of me. I gasped as he struck me so hard. So deep. He moaned and pushed in further, then slowly pulsating back and forth real easy. Teasing me. Taunting me.

I grew more wet as he sunk into me and rotated his hips. Picking up speed, he thrust harder and deeper, over and over. I was so wet he slid back and forth, hitting me so hard I could hear his pelvis slapping against my butt cheeks.

Our passionate session came to a jilted stop as we suddenly heard noises. People were coming back to the trailers; it sounded as if there were a couple of trucks in front of us. Weston released his grip from the left side of my hip and covered my mouth. Hovering over me, his lips came to my ear, "Shhh baby, don't make a peep." He continued to push himself inside of me, faster and harder. So hard I could barely take it. I held my mouth tight to keep the screams inside from coming out. He penetrated me on and on, further inside me, hitting my g spot. I moaned into his hand. I came again but more intensely, I had never had an orgasm like that before. It felt like an explosion went off in my stomach, a burst inside of me that couldn't be held back.

"Oh babe," Weston cried out as he came inside me, holding me steady and diving even deeper into me. I laid my body flat against the trailer, breathless, in mercy. His body relaxed, and he collapsed against my back, catching his breath. He slowly stood fully up and backed into the tree-line away from me, gently lowering my dress before reaching down to pull up his pants. I quickly pulled the straps up on my dress and adjusted my messy bun before stepping out of the torn panties that were entangled at my feet. Tucking his shirt back into his jeans and adjusting his belt buckle, he reached out his hand for mine, "shall we return, dear?" His grin was undeniable and adorable. I took his hand and smiled as he walked us back to the main arena.

We stopped by a food truck and grabbed some grub, seeing how we had just worked up an appetite, before taking out seats to watch the barrel races. A couple of hours had passed, and the rodeo was near closing time. Families began to filter out as the concessions and other vendors started packing up for the evening. Cattle and horses were escorted to their trailers for the night, and cowboys were taken into the beer tent for the 'last call.' Weston made a pit stop on our way out to say bye to his brothers and crew before heading to his truck. Arms wrapped around each other as we strolled to the car, embracing one another and walking in stride. Snickering about our sexual encounters and public indecency. Livestock wasn't the only thing being rode at this rodeo.

As we crept up closer to Weston's truck, we could see that his back left tire was flat. Not low, but completely flat. He released his snug grip from and threw his arms up in the air, "well shit, go figure. Karma for banging you in public," he laughed. I shook my head and giggled at him. He pulled down the tailgate and patted on the steel flatbed. "Come here," he said as he grabbed me around my waist and lifted me, Gently placing me on the tailgate. Kissing my nose and gleaming at me before stepping away to get a flashlight from the inside of the cab. "What the fuck?" Weston's tone went from cute and carefree to angry and confused as he walked around the right side of the truck to the passenger door.

I turned my head around, trying to see what he was referring to, "what is it, babe?" I asked, as I couldn't see what he was looking at.

"This tire is flat too," he said confused and somewhat suspicious.

Really weird," I replied

He reached into the car and grabbed the flashlight, switched it on, and lit up the tire. "Yeah, Meadow, this is really weird. I can see getting a flat by driving over something, but not both tires. And on opposite sides? I only have one spare. I'm going to call Evan and have him swing over here to give us a lift before he's gone. Hold on, babe."

While Weston called his brother, I hopped down from the truck. Grabbing the flashlight that Weston had just sat down while on his call. I lingered over to the back left tire, the first one we had seen when we were approaching. I squatted down and slowly circled the light along the tire tread. I ran my fingertips along the tire, following the light and feeling the ridges. Looking for a nail embedded in the tire or something to cause the flat. Shifting my body closer to the tire, I continued to inspect further back. Steadily, sliding my hands across, searching for a breach in the rubber. My fingertips grazed along until I came across a puncture in the wheel, an opening. I pushed further along until, ultimately, the edge of my fingertip slipped into the gash. No nails, no metal, nothing. There wasn't anything stuck in the tire, causing the air to leak out. It was a clear slit in the rubber. A nasty gash deep and rather long. My eyes widened as I stared at the tear. My pulse began to race rapidly. "Oh my god," I murmured to myself as I stood up and ran around the car to the other tire.

Hanging up his phone and tucking it in his back pocket, "What are you doing, Meadow?" Weston asked, watching me curiously as I dashed to the other side of the truck, "what's wrong, babe?"

My hands shook as I tried desperately to keep them steady, examining the other tire with my beam of light. My voice trembled just as my body did, "it's slashed; someone slashed your tire."

"What?!" Shocked and utterly confused, Weston walked over and bent down next to me as I proceeded to uncover the other tire's gouge, which was just the same.

"There, see it?" I aimed the light towards the gash in the tire and peered across the beam at Weston. His face turned from curious and inquisitive to concerned and angry. I'd never seen him with this look. His eyes followed the light, his brows furrowed, and his jaw was clenched as he studied the tear. His demeanor transformed abruptly from easygoing to tense, and his handsome face was now contoured with fury. He stood up, stretching his arm towards mine, holding my hand, and helping me to my feet. Just then, Evan pulled up behind us in his Chevy Silverado and hopped down from the cab. Evan was the baby of the boys; whatever his brothers did, he followed and always had. He was just slightly shorter than Tanner and Weston and had walnut-colored hair and chocolate-brown eyes. Evan was also the least serious of the brothers. Although he worked very hard, he played harder. Mischievous and good-looking, he was a handful even as an adult.

"What happened?" Evan asked as he emerged from his truck, cautiously approaching as he could see the disgruntled look plastered among Weston's face.

Weston sharply turned towards Evan, tossing his flashlight to him, "Tires are slashed."

Evan walked over to check out the wheel; shining the light among it, he spotted the rip, "holy shit."

Weston waved his arm, directing Evan to follow him to the other side, where he pointed out the matching slit. Evan lowered the flashlight to his side and looked over to Weston, "who would do this?"

My eyes leaped to Weston as soon as the question was raised: was he now thinking what I was?  All of these little events, occurrences, and inconveniences were clearly not just coincidences at this point. It was Ryan; it had to be Ryan. No one around here would do something so maliciously or have any reason to do so. I tried to convince myself that I was crazy and paranoid, overreacting to the last couple of days' incidents. But it wasn't just a hunch or assumption; it was real.  I could see in Weston's eyes he felt it, too. He was connecting the dots as well and beginning to believe it was happening. My worst fear had come true, and he knew it. Ryan found me, found me, and was here.

"Someone who clearly doesn't know who they are dealing with," he answered Evan with his voice cold and stern. Shifting his eyes and easing his tone to me, "Come on baby, get in the truck, let's get you home."

# CHAPTER 16

"I think it's time we called the police, Meadow; if it is him, then he could know where you work and where you live. Clearly, he's following you if he finds us at the rodeo." Weston had decided to stay with me tonight after what had happened. Evan dropped us off and told Weston he'd pick him up in the morning. We sat on the porch, drinking a glass of wine and talking through last week's events.

"But what if it's NOT him? What if we go to the police and explain the situation, and I get in trouble for arson or something? What if it's not him, and the police reach out to him? Then he does know I'm alive and where I'm at. I don't know what to do." I burst into tears and leaned forward cupping my head in my hands.

Weston reached over, stroking my back, "I don't know what to do either, babe. I don't like this, though; something is going on. Whether it's him or someone else, I don't feel like you're safe right now. I'm going to install some cameras around the property and outside of the cafe. Is that ok with you?"

I sat up and turned to him, wiping my face dry, "Thank you, that's a good idea."

"If something else happens though Meadow, we are calling the police." He said, "We will explain everything, and I promise it will be ok. You are the victim here either way. Don't worry, I got you." He smiled and tucked my weeping hair behind my ear. "Let's forget about it for now and take Shadow Boy for a walk." His eyes shifted to our feet where our adoring pup looked up with excitement and started wagging his little tail.

I giggled at the site; I wasn't sure who was cuter, Weston or the pup. I called it a toss-up and took Weston's hand as we led Shadow out in the yard for a late-night stroll. The sky above was so vibrant with stars it looked as if sprinkles of glitter fell from heaven. The moon was full and bright, scattering shimmers of light across the pond. The puppy frolicked through the grass, stopping and sniffing, pouncing and running. After a while, we decided to head in and get to bed; we were both exhausted.

I tossed and turned all night, having nightmares about Ryan. Dreams of terror, Visions of him finding me, attacking me, even strangling me. I woke up in a panic and cold sweat, my heart beating out of my chest. I looked over to find Weston peacefully sleeping beside me. I let out a sigh of relief; it was just a dream, and I'm safe. I crawled out of bed quietly, not to wake the cowboy, and got in the shower. As I ran the water, I began to undress. I slipped my shorts off and the waistband slowly grazed Ouch! What was that pain? I carefully slid my hand behind me and cautiously ran my fingers over the tender spot. My skin was raised in the area, and it was very sensitive to the touch. I turned around so that the back of me faced the full length mirror that was attached to the bathroom door. Stretching my chin over my shoulder so I could see my reflection behind me. As my eyes lingered, moving south to my butt, there it was, the source of my pain. The second battle scar.

An almost perfectly shaped hand print, multiple welts lining the design, purple and bruised. A bruise. I couldn't help but grin; with the distraction of the slashed tires, I almost forgot about our little rendezvous at the rodeo. I ran my hands softly against the print, tracing Weston's fingers with my own. Smiling at the memory of him smacking my ass over and over. Hard and aggressive. Why did I love it so much? The pain that came with his passion. Is it because before, I'd only known pain as punishment? This was different; it was a mark of lust and desire. Branding me in a sense, a certified claim of a cowboy. A bruise that now symbolized the craving for excitement and longing for sensuality as opposed to an emblem of fear and discipline. Some things change, while some stay the same. I didn't mind the bruises now; I looked forward to them.

I stepped into the steaming shower and in hopes of rinsing my anxious thoughts of Ryan's return away. As the hot water cascaded down my back, I relaxed my shoulders and held my head down. Letting the pebbles of water penetrate my shoulders with heat. My mind wouldn't stop racing, stirring with questions. Was it really Ryan? Should I call the police? What if I get in trouble for what I've done? What if he's notified and actually not involved? What if, what if, what if. I felt trapped again, as I did in my marriage. Scared and unsure of how to fix it, how to escape this intolerable feeling. Everything had been great for weeks, so smooth and natural. The fear had left me, and I was proud of how quick I was to look forward. The lesson I learned with Ryan is that life is too short not to be happy. Yes, I'm only 26 years old, but the point is that I left. I ran. I could have stuck around for years, terrorized and miserable for the rest of my life. Or, my life could have suddenly and tragically ended due to an "accident" that would have easily been at the hands of Ryan. It's hard to say what would have happened if I stayed. I got away once; I prayed he wouldn't find me. I didn't want to run again.

As I turned toward the water to rinse my face, the shower curtain gently opened behind me. I raised my chin and peeked over my shoulder; it was Weston. He entered the shower doe-eyed, cheesing, and with a full erection. His sun-kissed body only complemented his broad shoulders and chiseled physique. His eyes are stunning and sparkling, gleaming at me. The shower rained down on him as he stepped closer to me, glossing his tight body. I could get used to this kind of wake-up call.

"Good morning, baby. Do you need some help?" He stepped behind me, wrapping his arms around my stomach and kissing along my neck. I could feel him pressing against my ass, hard as steel.

I slowly turned to face him. Reaching my hand down and caressing his penis as he pushed closer to me. "I suppose you could be of some help," I said as I stroked him further. His hands ran from my stomach up to my breast, rubbing them under the water stream. Teasing and tugging at my nipples, licking my neck.

"Turn around," he whispered as he pulled my arm, guiding me away from the water, facing the back part of the shower. "Put your leg up here, babe," he slid his hand down my slippery leg until it reached the back of my knee, lifting it slightly and motioning towards the tub's corner edge. I lifted my leg as he said to and propped it up securely as he placed his hands on the back of my shoulders, pushing me forward and bending me over. I found myself in the same position as the night before, palms firmly planted before me to hold steady as I braced myself for him. He pushed inside me, stiff as a board, striking me hard and deep. I groaned as he slid back and forth, slow and with ease. Then he would go further, deeper inside me, holding a stance with a firm grip around my body. He would push his pelvis forward, penetrating more and more. I cried out as he slid his hands from my shoulders to my hips, holding me tight as he fucked me harder. He was strong and intense, passionate and sensual. The shower became hotter by the second, and it had nothing to do with the water's temperature.

He pulled out of me abruptly, spinning me around so that I was face-to-face with him. Grabbing the sides of my face and pulling me towards him, slipping his tongue in my mouth, biting at my lips. I ran my hands through his black, wet hair, tugging at the tips of his strands. His hands ran down my body until they found the bottoms of my butt cheeks. Squeezing my ass, lifting me up off the ground. My legs wrapped around him as he thrust inside me again, bouncing me off his pelvis. The veins bulged out of his tan and toned forearms, and his pecs flexed as he pounded me. His eyes were crystal blue and intensely focused on me, lusting for me. His face landed on my breast, sucking them and vigorously licking my nipples. My nipples were so hard, as if they had frozen over. Lifting my ass and then slamming me back down on him, striking me harder and faster with each movement. I held my arms around his neck, crying out as I came. He kept going, sliding in and out of me, hitting harder every time. Kissing my neck and chest, he held me tighter and closer to him as he finished inside of me. Crying out and pushing intensely inside of me one last time, as if he was savoring the final seconds of our passion.

The hot water poured over us as we held each other, panting endlessly, winded from our erotic encounters. Finally, Weston regained his strength and turned to shut the shower off. He held the curtain open for me to walk out and followed behind. After we got dressed, we headed downstairs, where I found Mom standing over the coffee pot and Shadow dancing at her feet. No matter how early I got up, she was always up before me. So, I plotted and planned ahead. She gets confused and overwhelmed with certain tasks, therefore I set things up for her ahead of time. Before I go to bed at night, I prepare the coffee and set the timer. That way, when she gets up, it's all ready, and I don't have to worry about her burning herself or forgetting to shut the water off. Mama also loves to greet Shadow first thing in the morning. I have a pretty strong suspicion that he likes it, too. When that chunky pup gets out of his kennel in the morning, he is hungry. I filled his water and food bowl the night before and placed it on top of his kennel, so in the morning, Mom just had to set it down on the floor. It helps everyone and buys me about 30 minutes longer to sleep.

"Good morning, mama!" I said as I snuck up behind her, wrapping my arms around her and squeezing her close. She grinned, and her eyes gleamed. She embraced my bear hug by placing her hands over my arms. Patting me gently along the top of my arms and embracing the back of my hands, holding tight. I planted a big kiss on her cheek; she laughed and pushed me away.

"Good morning, honey," she said, flashing me a smile and then swiftly shifting her focus back to the pot of coffee. It appeared that her last few minutes were spent rationing the proper amounts of sugar and French vanilla coffee creamer by the mess surrounding her red coffee mug. I try to let her be independent. I only step in to help when I physically see she needs it or she asks, which she actually does often despite her pride. I watched as she held her hand steady and reached for the handle, carefully sliding the pot off of the base and hovering over her cup. With perfect precision, she filled her mug and gently placed the pot back. A slight smirk smothered her face as if she was proud of her task. Nothing she was boasting about or even mentioning, just a little self-satisfaction I observed. It was adorable.

I spun Mama around in her paisley nightgown that tickled the top of her feet, meeting the fuzzy Ugg slippers I had sent her for Christmas. She smiled and waved her head, leaning in and kissing me on the cheek as she reached over for her cup of coffee and headed to the table. Newspaper was in hand, sipping her beverage, and the puppy was by her side. She was as happy as could be. I whipped up a quick breakfast of eggs, bacon, and toast, along with some fresh watermelon I picked up at the farmers market the day before. After we ate, I escorted Weston to the door, standing on my tip toes and kissing those luscious lips bye. He hugged me, smacked my ass, and trotted out the door. I started up the stairs to get ready when there was a knock at the door. I stopped in my stride and turned back down the steps to open the door. I assumed it was Weston and that he forgot something. I swung open the door, grinning, "Hello, Cowboy!"

He laughed and shook his head, "Hello you!"

Giggling, I asked, "Did you forget something dear?"

"I did," he said as he stepped forward directly in front of me. I stared up at him as he hovered over me. His eyes were still bright but more serious and focused, not as playful as usual. I studied his face and waited; what was he doing?

A sliver of a grin appeared on Weston's face just as his dimples shined through, placing his hands on my hips and pulling me into him. Lowering his head to reach my ear, he whispered, "I forgot to tell you something. I love you Meadow. I've always loved you."

My heart burst, and my face lit up. I wrapped my arms around him, pulling his lips to mine. Kissing him and running my fingers along his thick, black hair.

"I love you too, Weston," I whispered back to him.

He backed away from me, kissing my hand, before turning and walking to Evan's truck. My stomach filled with flutters and my heart with happiness. I don't think I ever had stopped loving Weston; we were just kids, and I didn't want a long-distance relationship. Who would have ever thought that we'd be together again? It's crazy how blinded I was before; everything I was searching for was already at my fingertips. I would never let it slip away again. I was infatuated with him, impressed by him, comforted, and oh so attracted. Every look and touch from him weakened my knees and raced my pulse. I couldn't get enough.

I skipped inside like an elated child, beaming with joy, my heart full. I had about an hour until I needed to open my coffee shop, so I ran through the house doing some quick chores. After I cleaned the kitchen up, I did a load of laundry and then checked on Mama and Shadow. My mom and pup were both planted in front of the TV on the sofa in the family room. The perfect little pair, my content couch potatoes. I smirked at the sight of them as I jogged up the steps to get ready for work. After I made my bed, I switched my yoga pants for cutoff jean shorts and threw on some light makeup. Tossing my blonde strands up in my usual glorified messy bun, I shut my bedroom door and headed back down the hallway to the stairs. As I shuffled down the stairs, I felt a slight chill in the air. Although the weather was warmer this time of year, it was still a little cool in the early hours. As I came to the landing of the staircase, I saw the front door was open. Wide open, pulling in the brisk morning breeze. I know I had shut it when Weston left, but the wind must have been a little stronger than I had realized, so I blew it open. Nonchalantly, I hopped down from the final step and pushed the door shut. It was time to go. I slipped on my shoes and grabbed my keys. Turning into the family room to say goodbye to my mom and pup, I stopped in surprise. No mom, no pup, just an empty couch.

# CHAPTER 17

"Mama! Shadow!" I yelled and began to walk from the living room to the kitchen, still not in sight.

Circling back around, I headed down the hallway towards Mama's room. There she was, sitting on the bed. She had changed out of her nightgown and was putting on her socks.

"Hey, mama, I'm going to work," I leaned down and kissed her on her forehead. "Have a good day."

"You too, dear. I'll see you later," she said as she stood up and gave me a hug.

Heading out the bedroom door, I called out, "Get a hold of me at the cafe if you need anything!" As I began to roam down the hallway, I stopped and spun around. Jogging back into the door frame of her room, "Hey, mama, where's Shadow?"

She looked at me blankly, and then her eyes wandered the room, "I'm not sure. He was just right here."

"The front door was open, mama. Did you let him outside?"

Her eyes squinted as I could tell she was trying to remember, "No, just earlier this morning."

"The wind must have blown it open then. I hope Shadow didn't sneak out."

Her hands began to fumble as she was now feeling worried about her little sidekick. "It's ok, Mom, I'll find him. Don't worry. Go sit down and relax."

I did a full walk through the house, with treats in hand, and called his name. Nothing. I really, really needed to leave for work. I didn't want to go without finding him, though, so I decided to run around the property to see if he was in the yard somewhere. After calling for him on the porch, I headed over to the shed and got on the Gator. I cruised down to the horse stables and all the way back around to the pond. Nothing. At this time, my stomach began to ache with fear that our little puppy had run away. As much as I wanted to find him, I needed to leave. I traded the ATV for my Acadia and sped off to work, my eyes sweeping the property as I made my way down the driveway and out on the road. I was scared that he might run out on the county highway and get hit by a car. Our home sat pretty far back from the road, so I was hoping he was somewhere on our land and would find his way back to the house. I'll call Mama later and check to see if he's coming back. I imagine he will return by lunchtime. You can tell he doesn't miss a meal with his round belly and furry fat rolls.

The shop was popping off from the jump. The rodeo was still in full effect, drawing all kinds of people to the area. It was so fun watching the variety of guests that would come into the establishment. Young children in cowboy hats and tassels geared up for the youth rodeo. The rodeo queen candidates posed for pictures in their rhinestones and denim. Old cowboys gathered around the table, drinking coffee and reminiscing about the 'good ole' days.' The energy was contagious, and everyone was friendly and kind. Plus, business was non-stop, which was obviously lucrative for me. The rush began to calm around 10:30 am as the crowd filtered out to the streets to watch the upcoming parade. The parade was just as big of a spectacle as the rodeo itself. I remember when I was a kid, I would stand along the road with my mom and dad, holding my Kroger shopping bag out in front of me and waiting for the loads of candy coming my way. It was always so much fun, one of my favorite things. It wasn't like any other parade. It was a spectacular event on its own.

The streets were lined with ATVs and tractors, and new farm equipment vendors were promoted. Horses stood forward, ready to march through crowds. These competition horses were unlike the ones that grazed these local fields. Their long, slender legs carried their broad, muscular torsos. Maines were sleek and styled, some with ribbons and bows that lingered throughout. Impeccable, trained, talented, and majestic overall. Folk dancers, a marching band, outfitted riders, and even horse-drawn coaches paraded the streets. Vintage vehicles cruised through, showcasing the rodeo queen nominees who were perched on the convertible deck lids of the cars. Brilliantly white teeth flashed the mass of people, and all graciously exhibited their royal waves. Handfuls of candy floated in the air, crashing at the feet of children standing by. The infectious sound of giggling spread through the mob as kids scooped up their treats and shoved them in bags. Grinning and gleaming, looking forward, arms outstretched, waiting for more.

I watched the beginning of the parade for a few minutes and then popped back into the shop. I still had a few customers I needed to check on. I took the coffee pot around the room, filling up cups and grabbing empty dishes from the tables. Everyone was content, so I took advantage of my quick break to call mama and check-in.

"Hey, mama, how's it going?" I cheerfully asked as she answered the phone.

"Hi, Meadow! It's good, just watching TV."

I chuckled, as I didn't really expect any other answer. She loved her soap operas. From 11 am - 1 pm, she was consumed. "Did Shadow come back, mom?"

"No, dear, I haven't seen or heard from him."

Ugh, my heart dropped. I was really hoping he had made his way back by now. "Maybe try stepping on the porch, mama, and calling for him? My poor baby is out there lost." I said in despair.

"Ok, Meadow, I will try. He will be ok, honey. He will come back home."

"Alright, mom, well, call me if you need anything. Remember the number to the shop is right there next to the phone, ok?"

"Ok dear, bye."

"Bye, mama." I hung up the phone and stood there for a second. Where could he be? He's still pretty little. I can't see him getting so far in such a short time. The front door could not have been opened for that long. I was only upstairs for about 15 minutes. How far could he really have gotten in that duration of time? I shrugged my shoulders and went back to work. Pups run off. He's a lab. His nose will help him find his home. I turned to walk back out into the dining room when they rang. That was quick. Shadow must have been near the house and heard mama call out for him.

I jotted over and grabbed the phone off the hook, "Hello, Coffee Couture!" I paused and didn't hear anything, so I repeated myself. "Hello, Coffee Couture." Holding my finger to my ear to help drown out the background noise filtering in from the streets, I pushed my other ear harder to the receiver. Listening for any noise on the other end. Faintly, I could hear breathing. Stepping back into my office, where it was quiet, the breathing sound intensified and became louder. My stomach turned as my heart leaped from my chest. Beginning to panic at the thought of Ryan on the other line, my voice quivered, "Hello?"

"How late are you open?" A deep, muffled voice emerged through the phone. I tried to swallow the lump in my throat. My hands trembled, and I could feel beads of sweat trickling down my forehead. It felt as if someone punched me in the stomach. I couldn't breathe. It was Ryan. With every chill in my bones, I knew it was him.

Taking a deep breath, I replied, "4 pm, sir."

"Thank you," the rough voice said as they hung up.

I collapsed in my office chair, slamming my body into the seat and bursting into terms. My entire body was shaking. I felt unsteady on my feet; it was as if the room was spinning. I leaned over, holding my head in my hands. Taking deep breaths in and out, trying to calm myself down, I slowly stood up. I glanced in the mirror, wiping the tears that drowned my face and fixing my bun that had become loose throughout the business of the day. I walked back out into the dining room, roaming the tables to see if anyone needed anything. As everyone was still hanging tight, I stepped back out front, where the parade was still in effect. I needed fresh air. I desperately needed fresh air. Stepping out a few feet from my front door, with my hands on my hips, I continued to inhale and exhale. Thinking, trying to think of what to do now. It had to be him. The notes of his voice hit my soul like a freight train.

I watched the performers before me and embraced the laughter of the children surrounding me. I felt comfort within the large audience as my nerves were pushed to capacity at this point. Scanning the crowd, my eyes followed the path of the parade. Observing the adoring bystanders as I soaked in the sun and caught my breath. As my eyes shot down the street, I caught an eerie feeling. Gravitating my sights back across the street from me, I saw him. There he was. Standing behind a family, peering at me. I kept my eye on him as he trailed through slowly, still looking at me. His hair, his clothes, the Ray-Ban aviators, it was him. My heart started to pound as I followed his steps. He came closer to the street. My chest began to rise as he was standing directly across from me. This is it. He's found me. Oh god, what have I done? He's going to kill me. He would have eventually killed me anyway, but now that I ran from him, I have no doubt in my mind he came here to do just that. Not taking my eyes off of him, I began to slowly step backward, etching closer to the shop door. As I cautiously backed up, he began to raise his hand to his face. What was he doing? Examining him instantly as I tried to make my way back in, I saw that he had removed his glasses. It wasn't Ryan.

I let out a gasp in shock and relief. I turned and jolted back inside the cafe. I'm losing it. Absolutely losing my mind at this point. My fear and paranoia were constant, and I couldn't shake them. I had to do something. I couldn't live like this forever, watching and wondering if he was coming for me. I had to confess. The time had come. I needed to go to the police. One way or another, this had to end. I called Weston and told him about the call and the mistaken sitting. He agreed with me that it was best to go to the police and take care of this. He suggested that mom and I pack a bag and stay with him this evening, just to be cautious, and then we could go file a report in the morning. I told him that sounded good and that we'd be over before dinner time. I loved how protective he was, endearing, and generous. I looked forward to a calm evening on his parents' ranch where I could breathe and relax momentarily.

Feeling better after my chat with my cowboy, I cruised the dining room and braced myself for the second rush of the day. Dozens of people flocked to the parade, filling the dining room instantly. This was a perfect distraction from the internal struggles I was facing and the overwhelming concern consuming me. I slapped a smile on my face as I greeted the crowd and served up lattes and croissants for the next few hours. Time flew by, business was booming, and it was nonstop until closing time. Finally, the mass dissipated as everyone was heading to the rodeo for the evening affairs, just in time for me to clean up and shut down for the day. After washing and putting away dishes, sweeping, mopping, and making the day's deposit drop, I was finally heading home. I was excited to grab mom and take her to Weston's for a sleepover. He has several horses on his ranch, goats, and even a couple of cows. She loves animals so much that she misses the livestock we once had. This would be a nice treat for her and perhaps help with her memory, too. They say there are certain triggers that help patients suffering from dementia remember past events or encounters. She was pretty sharp on a day-by-day basis, but if you asked her questions about things that occurred years ago, she really struggled to recall details and names. I was hoping the atmosphere filled with farm animals would maybe spark something deep inside.

I turned into our driveway, slowly rolling towards the house, scouring the area for a sign of Shadow. Calling out to him and whistling from my window.

"Shadow boy! Here, boy, come here, Shadow!"

Nothing, nowhere in sight. I was planning to get the Gator back out before our departure to examine the area further in hopes of finding our furry friend. I continued to call out for him until I reached the end of the driveway and parked my car. I decided to hop in the ATV right then to patrol the property. I wanted to take another shower after the busy day I had, so I figured I'd get this out of the way and hopefully locate the missing pup. I assumed that once found, he would be covered in mud, so I was prepared to get a little dirty with him before cleaning up. I revved up the engine and took off again towards the stables and shed, circling around the outbuilding and stretching my eyes to see far into the field. Nothing. Calling repeatedly for him with not anything as much of a whimper in the air. Frustrated, I headed back towards the house, riding behind it to trace the pond. Still no Shadow. Discouraged and saddened, I decided to park and go inside to get mama ready. It was getting close to her medicine time, and we needed to get packed and off to Weston's before dinner.

I stepped out of the gator, glancing to my left and right, still searching for the pup as I walked up the stairs onto the porch. Giving one last peak around the property before heading inside, I saw him. Shadow! He was right there, under the rocking chair on the porch. Oh my god! I spent this entire time scavenging the yard, and my sweet boy was right here all along. My heart was full again and gleamed with joy as I walked towards him.

"Shadow! Hey boy!" He continued to lie there, and he didn't even move when I clapped my hands together. Coming closer to him, I leaned down, "Shadow?"

# CHAPTER 18

"Shadow buddy," I squatted down to be near the pup, reaching my hand out to caress the top of his sleepy head.

He still didn't move, I nudged him a little and that's when his tiny body fell to its side.

I gasped and shrieked, "Shadow!"

I cried out as I took my hands and slid them under his helpless body, sweeping him up to me.

"Shadow, no, Shadow!" I wept, holding him tight to me.

He was dead, stiff, and cold to the touch. The playful soul that filled that body was now nonexistent. I held him, rocking him in my arms, heartbroken and devastated. I should have looked harder for him. He must have gotten into something bad that poisoned his small structure. Or perhaps he made his way over to the neighbors and took a swift kick from a horse. I felt horrible. How could I let him wander off? Mama will be so upset that her little shadow was no longer. I took a breath and soaked up my tears. I needed to go inside and tell mama about him. I knew just the place to bury him, too, near the bench by the pond. It's where he and his mom loved to sit. It was just so hard to let him go, but finally, I managed to lower the pup back on the porch and release him from my grip.

I leaned my body over to gently ease the pup onto the deck, slowly letting go and sitting my body back upright. As I began to stand up, I brought my hands to my face to wipe the streams of sadness away from my cheeks. Suddenly, I was frozen in stride as my eyes widened, focusing on my hands. My blood-soaked hands. Examining my palms and watching my fingers begin to tremble as I studied them. My chest began to pulsate with fear. I could see my heart pumping through my chest as I gazed down my body. I was covered in blood, my shirt and shorts saturated.  My breathing became rapid, and the knot in my stomach weakened my legs. I dropped to my knees, hands unsteady, reaching over to Shadow. Shaking wildly, I tried to keep still and examine him. As I eased my hands over his body, I pushed my fingers through his fur and along his torso. Letting out a horrific scream, I fell backward in shock and dismay. Pulse racing and my adrenaline inflated, mouth open, and eyes stunned with fear. His belly had been cut open. Not a scratch or even tear that would come from barbed wiring or a sharp stick. It was a huge gash. An intentional huge gash. One that would only be done with a blade, similar to the slits in Weson's tires. He's been here, Ryan has been here. My first thought was mama as I pulled my weak body from the floor to run inside.

I dashed across the porch to the screen door. As I grabbed the handle, something stopped me. What if he's still here? I closed my eyes and took a hard, deep breath, and then again. I opened my eyes and slowly opened the door, trying to keep it from squeaking as I pulled it open. Sliding my body in every so easily, tiptoeing until I was inside the house. Cautiously pulled the door shut behind me, bracing it with my hand so it closed quietly. I immediately glanced around the room, looking for mama. The lights were off, and it was silent. Just a small beam of light shined in from the front window, illuminating the room just enough for me to see it was bare. I crept across the room, lightly stepping towards the kitchen. As I approached the edge of the kitchen, I peeked my head around the corner, but there was nothing. Turning back around, I made my way down the hallway towards mama's bedroom.

I lurked down the dark hallway, keeping my back towards the wall and sliding closer to the bedroom. The door to her room was shut, but I could see the light coming through from the bottom. I held my body against the door, pressing my ear into it, trying to listen. I could faintly hear the television. Wrapping my hand around the doorknob, I slowly began to turn it as my other hand pushed it gently open. Easing my body into the opening, I stepped into her room. There she was, perched on her bed, watching the evening news.

My hunched shoulders dropped as I felt an ease come over my body, seeing that she was safe. I raced over to her, squatting down in front of her.

"Mama, I was worried about you. What are you doing in here with the door shut?" I asked as I leaned back, looking at her, placing my hand on her leg.

"Meadow," her voice shook, "why is there blood all over you? Are you ok? What happened?"

"Mama, listen to me. We need to leave. We need to go right now. I'm fine. This isn't my blood. I'll tell you later, but just trust me, we have to go."

"Meadow, is this because your husband is here?"

I felt as if someone kicked me in my stomach and knocked all the air out of me. I stared at her bewildered expression as my heart sank.

"What do you mean, mama?" I cautiously asked.

"He came here to Meadow. He said to tell you he will be back to take you home later."

Choking down my fear, I tried to remain calm despite my pulse racing and chest heaving. "When was he here, mom? What else did he say? Did you see him leave?" It felt at that moment as if the room began to spin, and the floor was ripped out from underneath me.

"Meadow, I didn't know you were married. Are you really leaving me, Meadow?" She began to weep and threw her arms around me, sobbing into my shoulder. "I don't want you to leave me."

Grabbing the sides of her arms and piercing into her eyes, she said, "Mama, I'm not going anywhere. I promise. Are you sure he left?"

"I watched him leave out the window. He had a black car with tinted windows."

"Ok, mama, ok." Holding her sweet, soft hand, "It's alright. I'm not going anywhere without you. In fact, pack a little bag for me and we are going to go stay with Weston tonight. Does that sound good? You want to go see all of his horses?"

She lit up, and a smile finally stretched across her face, "Oh yes, dear, that is perfect. Ok, I'll get my things now."

"Alright, mama, I'm just going to go give Weston a quick call and pack my stuff, too and then we are out of here, ok?"

Her voice finally relaxed with ease, "Yes, dear, I'll get ready now." I helped her stand up and grabbed a duffle bag from the top of her closet, tossing it on her bed.

"That should work. Just pack your nightgown and some clothes for tomorrow. I'll be back down here in 10 minutes." I planted a kiss on her forehead, "It's going to be just fine, mama, don't you worry."

I shot her a warm smile and then left her to pack her belongings, closing the door behind me. As I stood outside of her door, my strength crumbled, and I couldn't hold it any longer. With my back pressed against her door, I burst into tears. Sobbing uncontrollably, I thought I was going to hyperventilate. My chest heaved, and my palms were sweaty as I trembled with fear. I felt dizzy and nauseous. My legs were like jello. Trying to brace myself to walk down the hall, I was scared I would fall from the weakness overtaking my body. Choking back my tears, I began to place one foot in front of the other and trudge down the hallway. I just needed to make it to my phone to call Weston. Shit. My phone was in my car in my purse. I never brought it in. I began looking for Shadow as soon as I arrived home and never went back and grabbed it. Making my way down the hallway, it seemed like forever until it would end. I felt like the twins from the Shining, peddling down an endless path, searching for an exit. The walls felt as if they were closing in on me, narrowing the further I got. I kept going, trying to find strength in my steps.

It felt like an hour had passed before I reached the front door, looking to my left and then to my right, examining the room. It was silent and still. Somehow, the comfort and peace of the isolated countryside were now eerie and cold. Mustering up my strength and conquering my fear, I pushed open the screen door and rushed to my car. My eyes studied the area, roaming the yard for him. Nothing. The coast was clear, and the sun was setting. I needed to get out of here before it was dark. Yanking my driver door open, I dove in head first to reach for my purse. Shoving my hand inside my tote bag, my fingers stretched, searching for my phone. Nothing. I snatched my purse off of the seat and dumped it on the driveway. Watching as my things tumbled to the ground. I dropped to my knees, shuffling through everything. My wallet, sunglasses, gum, and no phone at all. Leaping to my feet, I went back into my car. Leaning over, stretching my body over the seat, feeling the floorboard for my phone. Nothing, it was gone. Wait, my keys. My keys were gone. I had turned the car off but left them in the ignition.  My panic grew more.  I shot my eyes forward to my house. The landline mama still had a landline. Herdling over my purse, I ran back to the house. Staggering over the steps to the porch, I tripped and fell. I fell hard. Smacking the bottom of my chin on the edge of the porch. I lay there, moaning as the pain was intense. I could feel it at my core. Holding my palms flat on the wooden deck, I pushed my body up. Soaking in the pain and wiping the blood from my chin onto my shirt, which was already stained from Shadow.

Shadow, my poor sweet Shadow. As I raised my body from the floor, I glanced over to Shadow's lifeless body. A flash of fright flooded my soul. Shadow was gone. Just residue of his blood marked the area he once laid. My eyes were transfixed on the spot, searching the rest of the porch. Blinking, rubbing my eyes, was I really seeing this? No, no, this wasn't happening. He is here. Here. My home, my safe space. Wobbly on my feet and short of breath, I ran up to the door, swinging it open and barreling in. Running to the kitchen, charging for the phone. Grabbing the receiver off the hook, I dialed 9-1-1 and pressed it to my ear.

"Hello, Hello! I need help, please. Hello?" Nothing. No dial tone, no one on the other end to hear me. No one to help me. Panic consumed me as I held the phone away from my ear, shaking undeniably. Trying again, but nothing. My chest was tightening as my eyes followed the phone line, finding the cord cut. I gasped as my hand released the tight grip I had on the phone, dropping it to the floor. I stood in shock, staring intensely at the cut line in front of me. My heart was racing, and my soul struck. I turned and ran out of the kitchen. Making a mad dash for the stairs. My dad had a gun, and when I moved mama back home, I took it out of her room and put it under my bed.

As I bolted up the stairs, I screamed, "Mama, stay in your room! Stay in your room, mama!!" I ran up the steps, taking them two at a time. Flying down the hallway, I busted into my bedroom. Falling to the floor at my bedside, I reached my arm underneath for the gun. Laying my face flat against the wooden planks, my eyes searching for the piece.

Fuck. It was far back, right in the center of the bed, and I couldn't reach it. I needed something to slide under the bed so I could pull the gun towards me. I sat upright, on my knees. Studying the room, searching for something long enough to reach it. I jumped to my feet and jogged over to my closet, grabbing a hanger. Racing back to the side of the bed, I hunched down and slid the hanger underneath. Stretching as far as I could, I tried to hook it and pull it towards me. I missed it. I repositioned my body, flattening my core to the floor. Reaching further and closer to the gun. It was just barely still out of reach. Wedging my shoulder underneath the bed frame, I extended my arm more and made another swipe for it. I missed it again.

Frustrated, I pushed as hard as I could and smacked the gun, shoving it further from me. Dropping my head in despair, I sat still next to the bed when the floor began to creak. My eyes remained down, staring at the floor. I didn't blink, and I didn't move. The floor creaked again. My breath became shallow, and tears began to emerge from my eyes.

My head shook back and forth, and my lip quivered as I whispered, "No." Trembling with fear, I raised my head up slowly. My eyes peered across the bed, where I knew my doom was waiting.

There he was. The devil in Prada himself. Ryan stood across from me, eyes dark and cold, piercing through me like sharp daggards. "Ah, my love, you don't seem happy to see me?"

# CHAPTER 19

"Stand up," he sputtered through his clenched teeth.

I shook uncontrollably as I tried to rise to my feet; my knees felt as if they could buckle at any moment. He stared intently, not taking his eyes off of me. Watching me fumble and fidget, amused by my discomfort and the fright consuming me.

"I have to say, Meadow, you have not been the best wife. What kind of woman runs out on her husband, commits arson to fake her death, and then runs back home to fuck a redneck?" He bowed his head and chuckled sinisterly, "You really played me for a fool. You know how much I hate to be embarrassed." Keeping his focus on me, he bent his knees, lowering himself in front of the bed. Reaching his hand under and pulling out my dad's gun, I pushed across the floor.

"What were you going to do with this Meadow?" Standing to his feet, showcasing the gun. Holding it before me, waving it in the air, examining it. Walking slowly around the bed towards me. Taking his time, torturing my soul with every step closer. "You almost had me, almost fooled me that you were really gone. You are just not as smart as you think, though, sweetheart, leaving behind a nice paper trail for me to find you."

My voice cracked as I squeaked out, "Please, no."

"Please, no, what Meadow? Don't hurt you like you hurt me? Is that what you're worried about?"   Coming closer to me, his face flushed with fury. His eyes were sharp and narrowed on me, nostrils flared, and the vein in his temple throbbing. Stopping before me, studying me up and down. Jaw was tense, and his forehead was covered in a blanket of sweat, resembling morning dew on the farm. Glistening profoundly while small beads trickled down his puckered eyebrows.

Stepping closer to me, placing his rigged lips near my ear, he muttered, "Or are you more worried about what I'll do to your mom and little boyfriend?"

"No!" I cried out, "No, please. I'm sorry, please don't hurt them."

He smirked with satisfaction as I wept, "Maybe I'll just leave them like that little dog of yours. It was so sad hearing it whimper while I ripped it apart. Almost the same joy I felt slashing your cowboy's tires."

"Please, Ryan, do whatever you want to me. Take me, take me back home. Just please leave them alone. My mama," I cried, "My sweet mama, she has nothing to do with this. Please just take me. Right now, we can go."

"Hmmm," his eyes wandered to the side as if he was suddenly in a trance, a deep thought. "Well, Meadow, the thing about that is, you're already dead." His eyes shifted focus back to me. Locking in on me, "How exactly do I bring a dead girl back home, Meadow? That doesn't even make any sense."

He held the gun up directly in front of my eyeline. Bringing it to my face as I clenched and closed my eyes. Running the barrel down my face, outlining my cheekbone, and tracing my lips. Slowly and steadily, watching the fear flood my body. He continued to press the gun against me, shifting down my neck and chest. Holding the gun firm to my stomach, watchin' me shiver, enjoying the terror he was inflicting on me.

"You know what's really nice though, my dear wife, is that since you're already dead, no one will ever know I killed you." He smirked and brushed the hair of my eyes. "You know, it is 'til death do us part.' I've been away from you this long and you were still alive. Sounds like a broken vow to me, one of many, I presume." He snarled and grabbed the back of my hair, yanking my head back while he shoved the gun against my throat. Pressing hard into my neck and glaring into my eyes.

Gritting his teeth and snarling, "After I kill you, I'm going to go downstairs and strangle your mom right in the bed she sits on. Then, I'm going to patiently wait here until your fuck buddy comes by to check on you. Where I will meet him with a bullet to the head and then be on my way back to Chicago. Best. Laid. Plans."

I whimpered with despair, "Please, Ryan, you don't have to do this." Choking on my tears, blubbering and pleading, "Please don't, I'm sorry. I'm so sorry for what I did, but you hurt me, Ryan; I couldn't take it any longer."

Fueled by my words, his face grew more intense, red, and furious. Pressing the gun harder into my neck and tugging tighter on my hair, he shouted in my face with spit spewing from his sharp tongue. "I was a great husband, Meadow, YOU, however, just couldn't resist defying me. Always defying me. If you just fucking did as you were told, none of this would have happened!"

He released his grip on my hair and lowered the gun just as he pulled back his arm and gave a swift, hard smack to my face. Hitting me so hard it spun me around and dropped me to the ground, where I landed on all fours.

"This…" He yelled as he kicked me in the side, "is all," kicking me again, "because of you!" Giving me one last jolt to the rib cage, knocking me off my knees and hands and on my side. Attempting to catch my breath and get back up. I pushed myself up to where I was back on my knees, trying to brace myself on the bed and pull my body upright. He punched me in the face, knocking me back flat to the floor. As he loomed over me, I began to crawl on my forearms, pulling myself along beneath him.

"Where do you think you're going, sweetheart?" Smirking and shadowing me as I tried to get away from him, struggling to lift my body up from the floor. As I finally forced my body back up on my hands and needs, I stumbled to my feet. Just as quickly as I stood up, he hit me again, throwing my body like a rag doll. I crashed into the trunk in my room breaking it into pieces, falling in it and a pile of junk and shreds of wood. Trying to pick myself up off the ground before he reached me, I struggled to plant my hands firmly enough to push my body up. So many things were under me I couldn't get a good grip. I felt around for something hard I could grab, something to hit him with. He was charging for me; I scrambled to get on my feet. Just as I was starting to rise, he grabbed me by the throat. Squeezing and pulling me fully to my feet. Pushing me against the wall, he released his hold on my neck. Once again, bringing his hand back to strike me, I uncovered the binoculars that had laid under me in the trunk. I wrapped my tiny hand around them just as he lifted me to my feet. With them in hand, I swung and smacked him right in the bridge of his nose. Beating him to the punch. He stumbled backward, dropping the gun and holding his hands to his face. Blood rushed through his fingers, dripping onto the hardwood floor under us.

"You bitch!" He screamed, lunging back at me. I stepped to the side and swung the binoculars again, striking him on his chin this time. Knocking him backward and into the nightstand. Knocking the lamp over, shattering glass everywhere. I grabbed the gun from the floor and bolted towards the door, slamming it behind me. Racing down the hallway to the stairs edge. As I turned the corner for the banister, my socks slipped against the wood floor, bringing me to a halt. I crashed hard, falling at the top of the stairs. The gun bounced out of my hand as I fell flat. I forced myself to my feet just as Ryan came out from the bedroom, infuriated, steaming full speed towards me. I shrieked and headed to the edge of the stairs; he grabbed the back of my shirt, pulling me back and down to the floor. I kicked at him as he tried to get on top of me, screaming and swinging my arms.

He pushed my flailing arms and legs aside and straddled me. Snatching the sides of my neck, choking me. I clawed and scratched at his wrist, trying to get him to release his commanding grip. I gasped for air. I could feel my chest getting tight; he was taking the life out of me. With every last bit of strength I had, I dug my nail into the back of his hand, tearing his flush. He groaned and loosened his hold just enough for me to turn my head and bite him in his hand. I bit down so hard, piercing his skin and drawing blood. He sat up in pain, screaming and finally breaking his clasp from my throat. I lifted my leg sharply as I pushed his body away from me, kneeing him right in the balls. He fell off of me, on his side, holding himself and yelling. Pushing my body further away from him, I hopped back on my feet. Snatching the gun from the floor, I rushed for the stairs. Just as I took my first step, he stretched his body out and lunged at me from the floor. Grabbing my ankle with his hand, tripping me, sending me tumbling down the stairs.

There I was, lying face down at the bottom of the staircase in my childhood home. My safe haven, my comfort and joy. Helpless and, once again, battered and bruised. I opened my eyes, staring at the grains within the wooden floor planks before me. The radiant light that once grazed the hardwood from the sun's beam through the windows had dissipated. The room is dark and cold, feeling much more like a haunted house instead of a farmhouse. It was a haunted house now, wasn't it? I was being haunted, not by a ghost but by my past. He found me, stalked me, terrorized me, and now he was going to kill me. All of this effort, energy, and time running from him just to end like this.

"Meadow?" A tiny voice squeaked nearby, "Meadow, are you ok?" It was Mama; she heard my body thumping down the stairs and slamming onto the ground. I pushed myself up to my knees, turning my body to look behind me. She stood at the end of the hallway, outside her room, holding her little duffle bag.

"Go back to your room, mama!" I shrieked, "Hurry, mama, now!" Shouting and waving my hands at her, "Please, mama, go lock your door, everythings ok! Go, now!"

Her eyes grew big, and her mouth opened wide, puzzled and

disturbed. Looking at me, her daughter, lying before her. Teary-eyed, she stared back at me and slowly nodded. She turned and shuffled back to her room, shutting the door behind her. My eyes shot back up to the stairs, where Ryan was sauntering down towards me. His face was grim and menacing, eyes hostile and fixed on me. His white shirt was now crimson from the splatters of blood drowning his shirt. His face was bloody and bruised; he was now my doppelganger. I hurt him. I could hurt him again. It doesn't have to end like this. I've fought this much; he's not going to kill me in my mama's house.

My adrenaline kicked in as I scanned the room for the gun that fell from my grasp when I fell. Jumping to my feet, I could see it on the other side of the staircase. Diving for it, I grabbed the grip of the gun and spun my body around. Turning my body just as Ryan leaped off the last 2 stairs, knocking the gun from my hand and punching me in my stomach. I doubled over, wrapping my arms around my guy, struggling to capture air. He reached down and grabbed the gun, bringing it up and cocking it back. Pulling me upright by the back of my hair and shoving me into the wall. Pressing his body firmly against mine, he raised the gun and placed it right under my chin. Suddenly, there was a knock at the door.

"Shh," Ryan pushed the barrel of the gun into my skin and whispered in my ear, "Don't say a fucking word or I will kill you." I trembled and sobbed, trying to quiet my quivering as he pressed his hand over my mouth. "Shut the fuck up," he snarled once again. His eyes focused on mine, intensely wicked and incredibly cold. Rage ran through his veins, and his heart pounded through his chest.

"Meadow, hey Meadow!" Weston knocked again on the door

and called out for me.

I tried to break free and cry out, weeping hysterically. Ryan pressed his hand harder against my mouth, gripping the sides of my cheeks, ensuring I couldn't speak. Jabbing the gun against my throat, he leaned back into my ear.

"Get rid of this fucker; you tell him you are staying home with Mom tonight and will call him tomorrow," Ryan spoke softly but sternly, never relaxing the gun gouging my throat. "If you say ANYTHING else, I swear I will shoot you dead right here and then your mom." The tears continued to stream down my face. I could taste the salt from them seeping through Ryan's fingers, covering my lips. "Do you understand?"

"Meadow! Meadow, open up!" Weston was still yelling for me, aggressively knocking. "Hey, you never came by. Is everything ok? I've been trying to call you. Why's your purse just out in the driveway? Meadow!" He banged on the door and shouted through the windows.

Ryan glared at me, "Don't fuck this up now. I'm going to move my hand from your mouth, tell him what I said. Calm yourself down, don't fucking let him hear you crying." Pressing the gun sharply under my chin now. "Now, do it. Say it."

I nodded again as he removed his hand from my mouth, shaking uncontrollably. I gulped the lump in my throat and licked my lips. Taking a deep breath in, I slowly exhaled out and held my emotions in place. Clearing my throat to speak clearly and not be choked by tears, I did what I was told.

"Weston, I'm sorry, but I'm not coming tonight. I just want to stay here with Mom tonight; I'll call you tomorrow." I spoke steady and with ease, controlling the pitch of my voice.

Weston sat quietly for a moment and then replied, "Will you just let me in Meadow, just for a second so I can check on you?"

Ryan slid the gun up my chin and grazed it over my cheek, raising it up slowly to the side of my temple. Scowling at me with his devilious torment, eyes enraged and lips perched, he pressed the gun so hard into me that I thought my eye would pop out.

Wincing from the pain of the barrel, I kept my tone stable as I continued to usher Weson away, "No, Weston, I don't feel like company. Please just leave. Please go."

Stammering and confused, Weston answered, "Do you want me to at least bring your purse to you?"

Ryan, frustrated by Weston's persistence, leaned in and growled in my ear, "Get him out now! My patients are running low. I'm about to just shoot him and be done!"

My eyes widened, and I nodded my head at Ryan. I had to get him out of here. I needed to be mean. I had to yell out and be mean to Weston and make him leave. My eyes filled with tears; I gulped and choked back my distress, "Leave now, Weston!" I snarled, "Take a hint and get the fuck off my property! Now! Go, Weston!" I screamed with as much force as my broken body would let me. "Go and don't come back!"

Ryan smothered my mouth with his hand once again, pushing so aggressively that my head smacked against the wall. We stood in silence, listening and waiting for Weston to leave. After a few seconds, his cowboy boots waltzed away, and the engine to his truck fired up. As he drove off, I could hear the rumbling of the gravel in the driveway. One of my most favorite sounds in the world was now leaving me. I cherished the rolling of his tires, shoveling through the pebbles on the ground, knowing he was close to me. Coming for me. The noise that filled my heart and excited my soul now shattered my inner being.

Once the roaring of the truck faded in the distance, Ryan released the gun from my temple and relaxed his hand from my lips. Gasping for air, my chest heaved, and my body shivered. Ryan put the gun in the back of his pants, grabbed me, and threw me over his shoulders.

"Now that was a good girl. Now, I just have to kill you and not him too." Ryan scorned as he carried me in the kitchen. I outstretched my arms, scratching at the door frame. Holding my arms locked, trying to hold tight. He shook his shoulder and forced me to release my grasp, carrying me fully into the kitchen. With one hand, he braced my body over his shoulder and then shoved everything off the kitchen table with the other one. My mom's vase full of fresh lily's smacked against the wall and crumbled into a thousand pieces. Paperwork and mail flew through the air like confetti, and a coffee cup smashed onto the floor. Launching me off of him, he threw me down on my back onto the table. Reaching behind him, he grabbed the gun that he had tucked into his pants and aimed it at me. Spreading my legs apart so he could position himself between them, he towered over me. Looking down at me, studying me. A gleam crossed his eyes as his tense jaw eased and a devilish grin prevailed. Lowering the gun to my knee and pressing into my flesh, he slowly slid the barrel up the inside of my leg. Ever so gently and torturous, gliding the gun against my skin, further and closer to my thigh. I shivered undeniably as the gun cruised my curves, my stomach full of knots, and my chest rapidly tightening.

"You know, it's a shame I couldn't have met your boyfriend. I'm curious to see what he's like. What exactly about him interests you? Did he know you were married?" Ryan's dark eyes locked on mine as he smirked, "Well, it doesn't matter now if HE knew you were married. You knew you were married, Meadow but still fucked a town hick, huh?"

I trembled and shook my head no, choking on my own tears and fears too much to manage any words.

"No, you didn't fuck a town hick?" Looking at me inquisitive and with a disturbing smile, "I think you did, honey. He stayed the night with you didn't he? Sounds like you have committed adultery."

Coasting the gun further up my thigh, he shoved the barrel in between my legs, jousting me with the pistol. I cried out, whimpering in pain and defeat. "Don't worry, darling, I'm going to remind you who your husband is. It's been a while. We should probably consummate again. No?" He ripped my shorts as I screamed and tried to pull his hands away from me. "Meadow, my hand is on the trigger; I suggest you let go now before I split your legs another way. Understand?" Gouging me once more with the shaft of the gun and then holding it upright, aimed at my head. "This is going to be fun, honey, like a little anniversary." He tugged at my ripped shorts, tearing the inseam apart. Watching me as he slowly unfastened the clasp on his belt and pulled his zipper down on his pants. I tossed my head back with anguish as the tears rolled down my puffy cheeks and shut my eyes.

# CHAPTER 20

Even with my eyes closed, I could still see down the barrel of that gun. I laid there, weak and battered, with him prevailing over me. I tried to fight; I tried to save myself. I tried to save my mom and Weston. It was over, done. I had no more fight in me. He was a man who always got what he wanted. He wanted to kill me, and now he would. No one would ever know I'm already dead. The town folks will think I just went back to Chicago, and no one will believe my mom's story about Ryan being here. They'll think she's confused and "mixing things up again" if she's still alive to tell.  He's rich and powerful and probably already has an alibi lined up. I pictured my mom's sweet face and sobbed at the thought of her finding me dead. Or worse, what if he kills her too? This was all my fault; I should have never ran. I should have never come here.

"No!" I cried as he pulled at my panties, trying to tear the waistband and rip them off. "No, please, no!" I screamed and pleaded as I raised my head up and looked at him.

"Shut the fuck up bitch, one more word, and I'm shutting you up for good!" His bloodshot eyes widened, and his pupils were dilated. He waved the gun at me and cocked his head to the side, holding his fixation on me with his dark, dead stare. I panted, trying to catch my breath as the nerves in my stomach intensified, my body rattling against the wood table. He leaned his body over mine, "Shh baby, you should be more excited to see your long-lost husband." Revealing a vile smirk before spitting on me. Raising his body back up, his wrathful demeanor cascaded over my body. Wiping his venom from my face, I held my head up and glared back at him.

"Fuck you, I want a divorce." I snarled as I swung my arm up and knocked the gun from his hand.

Furious, he gritted his teeth and frowned his brows, lunging on top of me. Mounting me and wrapping his blood-covered hands around my neck. "You bitch!" Just as he began to unleash his rage and strangle me, Weston busted through the backdoor with a vengeance. Crashing into the room and grabbing Ryan by the back of his shirt, pulling him off of me, and throwing him to the floor. Shocked and surprised, I sat up, gasping for air, and quickly hopped down from the table. I stood with my back towards the wall, scanning the room for the gun. It must have slid under something in the kitchen, I couldn't see it anywhere. Ryan, awkward and unsteady, rose back to his feet and charged at Weston. Weston's stance was strong, his forearms bulged, his eyes intense and fueled with anger. He caught Ryan with a straight right, knocking him back against the kitchen sink. He stumbled to keep his balance, knocking over dishes as he tried to grab the counter to hold himself upright. Weston marched back over to him with his fist clenched, punching him again and again until Ryan slid down to the floor. Weston hunched over and hit Ryan one more time with his undeniable brute force, knocking him fully over to where he was laying flat on the linoleum.

"Meadow!" Weston turned to me, "Are you ok?"

"Yes, I'm fine; my dad's gun is down here, I'm trying to find it," I shouted as I leaned down, looking under the baker's rack for the pistol.

"Where's your mom, Meadow?" He asked as he rushed over to me, wrapping his strong, loving arms tightly around my waist. Pulling me into his body, hovering over me, and holding me tight. I couldn't stop shaking even in the comfort of his warm embrace.

"She's in the bedroom; she's safe. He took my cell phone and cut the landline, I couldn't call out. He took my car keys, I was trapped." Still trembling, I buried my face in his broad chest, sobbing uncontrollably. It's like all of the adrenaline left my body, and the fear was pouring out through my tears.

Stroking my back with his heavy hands and trying to calm me with his gentle tone, he said, "I saw the blood on the porch when I came by earlier, I knew something was wrong." Squeezing me more, "I'm so glad you're ok. I called the cops; they should be here soon. Go get your mom, let's get her out of here and in my truck." He kissed me on my forehead and released me to go get Mama.

I made a mad dash through the kitchen, barely glancing at Ryan's lifeless body slouched in front of the sink. Sprinting down the hallway towards my mom's room as if I were in a relay race, I burst through her door.

Her eyes were bright and wide, "Oh, Meadow!" She cried out, "You're ok! Oh, you're ok!" She staggered up from the bed with Dewey eyes and draped her soft hands around me. Hugging me and stroking my hair with her tiny fingers, her chest heaving against mine from fright.

"It's ok, mama, I'm ok. We have to leave now, though. Right now." I comforted her with a tight squeeze and then backed away.

Grabbing her bag off of the bed, I led her out of the room and down the hall. Weston was already waiting at the front door; his truck was grumbling out in the driveway. Our getaway vehicle. Our escape from this nightmare. Through the screen door, I could see the ambient light from the moon and hear the crickets chirping in the grass. A subtle distraction from the terror that loomed over my farmhouse this summer night.

Weston opened the storm door, extending his strapping arm to Mother, guiding her out and to his truck. As he helped her down the stairs of the porch and up into his truck, I took a step back to peer into the kitchen. I could still see Ryan's shoes and the cluster of kitchen utensils and dishes scattered among the floor. He was still knocked out from Weston's powerful blows. I stepped back again and turned towards the kitchen doorway, shifting my body, peaking and prowling the area for the gun. Where did the gun go? Even though Ryan seemed to be unconscious, I still wanted the gun. Ever so gently, I glided my way back into the kitchen. Eyes alert and scanning the perimeter for the pistol. Cautiously passing by Ryan's bloody body, I tiptoed towards the dining table steadily searching under and behind it for the gun. Suddenly, I froze with fear as I heard lurking behind me. Stepping closer and quicker towards me, I spun around in panic. It was Weston.

"What are you doing babe?" His eyes were curious and distressed, he tugged at my arm, "let's go Meadow. Police will be here soon, let's just hurry and get out of here." His strong, copper-toned hands, now stained with Ryan's blood, grabbed the sides of my battered face. He kissed me and grinned, "It's over now, come on."

Just as I looked up into those bold, beautiful blue eyes of his, I could see a shadow rising behind him. "Weston, watch out!" I screamed as Ryan came from behind. A wrath of vengeance swept across his grisly face. Eyes black as night and enraged. Raising his arm and revealing a kitchen knife he grabbed from the floor, he heaved the blade into Weston's side.

"NO!" I screeched as Weston stumbled and then fell to my feet. "Noo!" I bellowed out as my heart sank, and I felt a crushing blow to my soul. Staring down in my despair at Weston, I was overcome with anger. This was my fault. All of this was my fault. I led him here. I led this psycho back to my hometown and put everyone in danger. My heart was broken, and my head was spinning. I raised my gaze from my hero to the villain, his merciless eyes locked on me.

"You're next, you fucking bitch!" Ryan growled, teeth clenched. Lunging at me and swinging the blade, I leaped back as he slashed my shirt with the knife's tip. He lost his balance and stumbled into the dining table. I took advantage of his disadvantage and wobbly feet and hurled over my fallen cowboy, darting out of the kitchen. With Ryan hot on my heels, I made a sharp turn around the kitchen door frame, snatching the lamp off the end table in the foyer. Positioning my back against the wall and holding steady, keeping my body out of site until Ryan emerged into the room. He charged in from the kitchen just as I swung the lamp with all of my strength, bashing the light against his face. The blade fell from his hand as he was stunned and surprised. I struck him again and then dropped the lamp, running for the knife that had slid into the corner. Ryan screamed and raised his hands to his face, trying to weed out the shards of glass now embedded in his skin. Struggling to see and displaced, I snuck past him and stretched my arms out below him, desperately grabbing for the knife. It was just barely out of reach, trying to dodge his aimless wandering as he was still trying to clear his vision, I clutched the handle of the knife. Finally, feeling a short sense of relief, I began to pull the blade towards me when I was tackled to the floor by Ryan. The knife falling from my grasp to the ground once again.

"Bitch!" He wailed as my back smacked the hardwood for the second time that night, so hard my body felt momentarily paralyzed. My head bounced off the floor like a tennis ball, and sharp pain spread through to my core. I moaned and tried to move as Ryan hovered over my still and stiff body, gripping my throat with his shaky hands. "Just fucking die!" He snarled as he tightened his hands around my neck, squeezing and choking me ferociously. I tried to pry his hands off, tugging and scratching at his fingers. Clawing the backs of his hands and tugging on his shirt. My breathing became shallow, my site fuzzy. I was becoming weak and struggling to kick my feet any longer. It felt like I was in the deep end of a swimming pool, fluttering my limbs and moving nowhere. Submerged and drowning. Laying there helpless and hopeless, enchanted by the chandelier above me, studying the twinkling of the lights as if they were the sun above the water. Feeling faint and my hands falling to my sides in defeat, I continued to glare at the gleam when suddenly an eclipse crossed my site. The radiant glow became seemingly covered, only illuminating an outline of a figure. It was Weston.

Weston had emerged from the kitchen, towering above Ryan's unsuspecting body that was draining the life from me. His eyes tense and sharp, Weston reached down, snatching Ryan's shirt and hauling him off of me with brute force. Propelling Ryan's body across the floor like a rag dog. Strutting towards Ryan, Weston hiked his leg back and kicked him in the ribs as if he was punting a football in high school once again. Dropping down to his knees, Weston grabbed Ryan by the throat, slamming his head against the floor. Again and again, choking him furiously as he just had me. The veins bulge from his rugged hands, and his knuckles turned white as he strangled Ryan. Weston straddled him, his masculine back facing me as testosterone engulfed his body, and he continued to choke Ryan. Fuming with intensity and anger, squeezing his neck harder. Ryan's hands waved with fury, yanking at Weston and pulling at his wrists, trying to remove his python grip. Digging his hand into Weston's wound and gouging his exposed flesh, Weston howled in pain and rose up, releasing his grip. Ryan shoved Weston off of him and climbed to his feet. Kicking Weston in the face and hurling his body back against the side of the staircase.

"Weston!" I cried out as Ryan glared across his tattered body at me, chest puffed and eyes flaming with rage. Ryan bolted towards me, hopping over Weston; I turned and ran for the knife, diving on the floor. Ryan snagged my ankles, dragging my body away from the blade. Stepping before me, kicking the knife across the room under the couch. I scrambled to my feet, racing back into the kitchen, searching for the gun. Just as I spotted it, wedged under the corner cabinet, Ryan pulled my hair from behind, yanking me to the ground. Standing above me and peering down, he stomped on my stomach, knocking the air out of me. Rolling over, gasping for air, and holding my gut, I tried to stand. Unable to speak and struggling to get up,

Ryan forced past me and grabbed the gun. Turning back towards the foyer, he marched past me, shoving me back to the ground. Pushing my unsteady body up, I ran behind Ryan as he was walking out of the kitchen, launching my body onto his back as he made his way towards Weston. Wrapping my arms around his neck and tieing my legs against his torso, I leaned in and bit the side of his neck. I bit hard, tearing into his flesh and ripping it away, tasting his blood and hearing his agonizing scream as he twirled around, trying to toss my body from his.

We spun in circles, knocking into furniture and bouncing off the walls until he finally flipped me over his shoulders into the foyer table. Crashing into a custom creation, my dad built 30 years ago, I tumbled to the floor along with the vintage piece. The crystal vase shattered around me, picture frames flew in the air, and the drawers fell out from the table. Pens and paper scattered on the ground, along with my motionless body and the gun. Weston lunged for the gun, blood pooling from his side, saturating his denim wranglers. His face flushed and eyebrows raised, arching his body upright to snag the pistol when Ryan kicked him in his chin, sending his back on the ground. Ryan's menacing grin smothered his face once more as he stood in victory over Weston, aiming the gun at his fallen body. I shuffled my arms aimlessly along the floor, searching for something to stop him. Something to hurt him.

"See Meadow," Ryan bellowed, "this is what happens when you don't listen." Cocking the gun back and stepping closer to Weston, and in my vision, I scanned the ground in desperation. A glimmer peeked out from a pad of paper, a shine peering at me. My eyes widened as I extended my arm past Ryan's foot and stretched my fingers to grasp the metallic shine before me. It was the pocket knife Bob, the car dealer, gave me. My face lit up as I pulled the chrome-plated gadget towards me. Popping open the blade, I stared at my reflection, gleaming at my steel eyes, before jabbing the knife into Ryan's calf.

"Ahh!" Ryan screeched as the pain soared through his body; he threw his head back, flooded with anger. He howled like a wolf to the moon. Spinning his body towards me, he kicked the knife from my hand and then pressed the gun to my forehead. Defenseless and on my knees, looking up at the devil, I realized I had lost the battle.

Ryan smirked as he stared down the barrel of the gun at me, "This is it, dear; you wanted to play dead, and now you are dead." I took one last glance at Weston's still body across from me, a deep breath, and shut my eyes.

Bang.

I screamed and fell over, covering the back of my head with my hands. Burying my face into the ground, trembling as tears balled down my face. Panting and squinting my eyes shut, I remained there, rocking gently back and forth. Wait. Wait, I'm not hurt. He didn't shoot me. I popped my eyes open and lifted my body up. Ryan was lying in front of me with a bullet wound in his chest. I gasped at the site, covering my mouth in disbelief. Confused and shocked, I raised my eyes up towards the front door. The sheriff was in the doorway, tucking his gun back in his holster. I cried out with relief, dropped my shoulders, and hung my head.

"Are you ok, Meadow?" Sheriff Bradford said as he came towards me, his deputy right behind him and two more guys coming in from the porch. I could see the dazzling red and blue lights in the background, lighting up the driveway like the 4th of July. The men barreled in, snatching Ryan off the floor and placing cuffs on his wrists before hauling him outside. "Get him to the hospital, but keep him cuffed to those bed boys," the sheriff ordered as he continued to saunter towards me. Reaching his hands out to help me up, he asked again, "Dear, are you ok?"

I nodded my head and managed to swallow the lump in my throat enough to answer, "Yes." Then I shot my sites to my beloved boyfriend, lying in the aftermath.

"Weston!" I yelled as I looked across the room at him and rushed to his side. "Weston was stabbed; he needs help." I leaned down beside him, stroking his soft black hair and kissing his chiseled cheekbones. "Are you alright? Weston, are you ok? I'm so sorry!" I couldn't choke back my tears; I thought I was going to lose him.

"I'm ok baby, I'm ok," Weston grinned and wrapped his arm around me, pulling me into his chest. Whispering over me, "It's all over, babe, it's all over."

# CHAPTER 21

## 3 Months Later

It was autumn in Kentucky, and the leaves were vividly brilliant, decorating the sumacs and dogwoods with shades of red and purple. The rich forest covered the mountains like a warm blanket, trickling stunning pops of orange and yellow throughout. Harvest season was upon us, farmers tended to the fields, and the laughter of children filled the pumpkin patches. American flags waved high above the tractors, and cattle grazed meadows of vibrant wildflowers. The fall foliage was spectacular and mesmerizing, an endlessly enchanting sight. I missed this. For six years, I missed the sun setting over the red barn, brightening the dwindled wood with the sun's gleam. The mist of the morning dew covered the emerald grass and the sweet sounds of birds singing in the air. I was here now, and that was all that matters. Sometimes, we become so clouded by a dream we can't see we are already living one.

It had been 3 months since Ryan came to turn my dream into a nightmare. He failed. He was finally gone, and I was free at least. Ryan was arrested and charged with attempted murder, stalking, and home invasion. The judge added a sweet cherry on top and granted me a default divorce, which also allowed me to change my name back from Mrs. Cooper to Meadow Williams. I couldn't be any happier; the devil was gone, and I was walking on clouds as if heaven was right here on earth. Weston healed up just fine, my cowboy-turned-knight and shining armor. I will be forever grateful for him; who knows what would have happened if he hadn't come back for me and Mama? My sweet mama, I felt so horrible for what she had to see, and just watching the terror in her eyes broke my heart. It was behind us now; we were safe, settled, and secure.

I didn't have the heart to tell Mom about the pup, so we got a replacement Shadow and told her a farmer had found him lost in a field. It worked. She was ecstatic to have her little buddy back; they looked so much alike that I, at times, forget it is a different puppy. Weston also got her two horses from the auction and cleaned up the stalls. Every morning, Mom would get up with Shadow and walk to the stalls, and watch me feed the horses. Sipping her coffee and shuffling around in her nightgown was my favorite part of each day. Watching the sunrise illuminate her soft smile, her endearing eyes captivated by the majestic creatures. It was breathtaking to me, watching her come back to life more each day. She named her horses Laverne and Shirley and admired them daily, calling them her "babies." The property looked gorgeous; Weston had put a ton of work into patching the fence, staining the porch, tending the pond, and also tilled up a little garden area for Mom. She was living her best life, and I loved every minute of it.

I was also living my best life. My bruises from my battle with Ryan were long gone, along with my fear. I was happy and content, comfortable in my own skin. My roots pulled me back in, soaking my soul with hope. The cafe was amazing, thriving, in fact. It was my sanctuary, my second home. I took so much pride in my sweet little shop and truly enjoyed it. I think being isolated for so long in Chicago gave me a desire for socialization and a need for satisfaction. Weston set me up with an adorable trailer so I can take the shop on wheels.

That's right, Coffee Couture Mobile right here in Versailles for all of your private event needs. Not how I pictured my career turning out, but I didn't see it in full color back then. I went from broken to built. Abuse is a crazy thing; what people see are the bruises that cover your body, but they don't see those consuming your heart. My heart was no longer bruised; it was healed and full. Open. Wide open and taking all of Weston in. There is a pot of gold at the end of the rainbow; you have to run for it to find it, though.

Looking back now, I ask myself why I didn't leave sooner. Why did I stay for so long? Why did I let him break me down and hold me back? Fear ultimately, but also shame. No one wants to tell people they failed at something, especially their marriage. No one wants to share horror stories from their husbands' hands or be seen as a victim. We wait for change and hope for it. Think maybe they will be different one day, maybe you can avoid upsetting them. Form to fit their expectations and grant their needs before your own. That isn't love. That isn't marriage. It's anarchy. I believe everything happens for a reason to each of us. Perhaps for me, I wasn't strong enough to leave sooner. Maybe I wouldn't have been smart enough and planned well enough. It was a total success as he seemingly found me, but it was a start. A leap. Six years of enduring pain and suffering, disgrace, and despair pushed me to finally run. It wasn't soon enough, but at least it wasn't too late.

Gazing out the window of the cafe as I waited on my final table to finish up their glazed donuts and gossip, I couldn't help but grin to myself. The sun was shining on the town streets, illuminating an abundance of mums bursting with brightness that lined the sidewalks. Boutiques buzzing, and adoring children raced to the door's edge of the ice cream shop across the street. It was a vision. One that never got old. Chicago was cold and corporate; streets loomed black no matter how strong the sun's rays were. People didn't hold the door open for you or smile when you passed by. The city culture didn't admire values and family as much as they did money and power. Southern hospitality, the love of my life. Well, one of them. My grin stretched to a smile at the site of my cowboy walking up to my door. Talk about a vision; he was a vision. There wasn't a wildflower or panoramic mountain view as spectacular as the site of Weston Ridge.

The skies light beamed onto his radiant glow, his summer tan still pronounced and golden. His wide chest and masculine arms swung along his long, chiseled frame. His glorious physique was as striking as his handsome face. His blue eyes lit up his prominent cheekbones and defined jawline, and when his dimples popped, my legs quivered. The way he tipped his cowboy hat when someone walked past and winked at kids running by made my heart melt. He was a gentleman and a savage, rugged and romantic. And he was all mine. Strutting right towards me, boots in stride and that mischievous smile on deck.

"Well, hello, Mr. Ridge; what can I do for you?" I asked with a cheesy grin as he took a seat on the barstool at the counter in front of me. Leaning in to kiss those luscious lips of his. Once and then twice.

"Well, I'm better now," he chuckled as he grabbed a menu and began to look it over.

"Why are you reading that? You know everything we have?" I laughed, tugging at the menu.

"Actually, the reason I look at the menu every day is to see if there are any updates. You know, any new additions."

"Ahh," I nodded, "I see; what addition specifically is it you are seeking dear?"

Shifting those piercing peekers of his over the menu at me, "You know what I'm looking for, Meadow, don't tease me now."

I knew exactly what he was talking about but it was more fun making him say it. After scanning the paper once more, he reluctantly sat it down with disappointment. "Just thought you were going to add 'Dinner with Weston' to the menu. Guess I'll just write it for everyone..."

Bursting out with laughter, I tossed my head back and then flirtatiously yanked the menu from the countertop, placing it back on the stack of others. I leaned my body across the bar, slowly and sensually. Caressing and covering Weston's hands with mine. "Come closer," I whispered to him. Tickling his broad, roughneck knuckles with tender touches from the tips of my fingers. He graciously and subtly moved in just a smudge.

"Come just a little closer, baby," I whispered delicately. He moved in closer, much closer in face, almost lip to lip. His cologne tickled my nose, and his eyes locked on mine. "I can't add you to the menu, Weston; I don't want anyone else to order you. You're all mine." Tipping my body in closer, I kissed his cheek and then slowly moved my lips up, grazing along his stout jawline and finally nibbling on his ear.

He blushed and smiled, "Well, are you hungry now, Meadow?" He laughed and shrugged his shoulders, panning the room. "I think it's time for you to close up, dear; we're skipping dinner tonight and going right for dessert." I giggled and nodded, leaving the counter; I headed over to my old ranchers, gave them their bills, and sent them on their way.  I followed them to the door, thanking them for their patronage, closing and locking it behind them. Just then, the lights turned out. The sun was lowering, and only a subtle shine came through the windows, lighting the front of the cafe and dimming the rest. I turned around to see the outline of Weston's back near the light switch. Looking like the silhouette of the Marlboro man, complete with Durangos and Levi's. He flashed a smile at me from across the room, lowered his straw hat, and placed it on the counter. Raising his arm up and motioning for me to come to him. I sauntered across the floor towards him, enchanted and excited. Watching him look at me turned me on; the way he stared at me gave me butterflies.

Approaching him, I stood short of his tall build, just falling in line with his broad chest. Gazing up at him, I let my fingers trace the buttons on his plaid shirt before taking my time to unbutton each one. Eventually revealing his sculpted torso and ridged hip line. Pushing his shirt off of his shoulders, I slid it down his arms and watched it fall to our feet. Running my hands up his now bare arms, I embraced every muscle and bulge, touching him softly and slowly. My fingertips followed along his stout physique, lingering along his chest and crawling lower. His breath became heavy; his eyes were full of spark and lust, those lips wet and wicked. I wanted to bite them, suck on them. Pull at them. I turned my eyes away from him, looking down, watching my hands explore his body. Grazing his abs softly and then trickling down to his distressed denim. At last, reaching his belt buckle, I wrapped my hands around the brass latch and gently unhooked it. Taking my sweet time pulling down his zipper, kissing along his ample chest, testing his patience, and teasing him.

Drifting my eyes back up to meet his, I slid my hand down his jeans and gently stroked him. He was already hard, long, and stiff as a board. Running my hands along his shaft, up and back down. Flickers of light danced in his intense eyes from the low sun sprinkling in through the windows. Eyes engaged on me as if he was stuck in a trance. His lips pouting and wet, running his hands through my blonde locks, whispers of moans creeped out his lips. Circling the tip of his penis ever so softly with my fingertips and then slipping my hand further down his pants. Wrapping my fingers around his rock, feeling his pulse, and he hardened even more with each pump of my hand. He couldn't take it anymore.

Grabbing the back of my hair, he pulled on my strands, forcing my neck back and face up. Bending his neck down to reach my small exterior, his lips caught mine. Pressed against mine, firm and passionate. Easing his wet tongue in and stroking against mine, biting on my bottom lip as he released his grasp. Tugging on my hair, it hurt just enough to feel good. Excite me, make me want more. Grazing his teeth along my neck, nibbling on me, kissing my skin, and taunting me. I pushed his jeans past his hips and, let them drop to the floor, and pushed my body closer to him. Pressing my pelvis against his hardwood, feeling him against me, rubbing myself on him, I became hot. He was irresistible and sensual. I embraced his flexed figure against mine and drove my hands up his broad back. Squatting down to my level, his strong hands gripped my butt cheeks, and he effortlessly hoisted me off the ground. Lifting me up and placing me on the countertop. Pushing my legs apart, he wedged himself in between them and grabbed me around my waist. Kissing me with his tantalizing tongue and lips so luscious. He laid me back on the counter with my legs hanging off, dangling against the cold bar. Vulnerable and open. Anxious and awaiting his next move.

"Just stay there for a minute, dear." He whispered as he took a snug seat between my thighs on a barstool before me. "Now, you wouldn't add Weston to the menu so I'm going to improvise."

I giggled as I felt him push my legs further apart and wedge himself closer to me. It tickled as his 5 o'clock shadow on the 5 o'clock hour brushed against my skin as he kissed along my inner leg. His soft lips gently tapped against my flesh, teasing me more and more. Dancing along my skin ever so softly and sensually.

"Oh yeah?" I grinned as I stared up at the ceiling while my cowboy had me spread eagle before him. "How so?" I flirtatiously asked as I ran my hands through his thick hair, pulling gently at the ends.

Raising his head up and flashing a smile that I could feel even though I wasn't looking at him, "I'll just put Meadow on my menu. I am hungry." He put his head back down and tugged on my shorts with his teeth, sending me into a fit of laughter.

"YOU don't have a menu, baby; this is my cafe," I teased as I continued to caress the back of his head and stroke his thick hair.

His fingers began to drift up my leg, lingering along the edge of the fabric. Shifting his hands up to the sides of my shorts and tucking his fingers inside the waistband, I raised my pelvis up off the countertop. Allowing him to withdraw my shorts and slip them off my legs, pulling them past my feet. Sitting my butt back on the bar, he wrapped his arms under my thighs, pulling himself into me. His mouth kissed me once again, much further south this time. His wet tongue tasted me, tracing along my insides. Gliding smoothly back and forth, with more pressure each time. Flicking me with the fierce force of his tongue, again and again, faster and harder.

Raising his head from between my legs, he reached his arms up and grabbed my hands. Snatching me off of the counter top and spinning me around. He shoved me forward from the back, leaning my body face down on the bar. Gripping the sides of my hips and pulling my ass towards him, he slid inside of me. Hard, deep. Grinding inside of me, he moved his hands up the sides of my arms and squeezed tight. Holding onto me as if I were a headboard, using my arms to thrust himself in and out of me with force. I screamed and moaned, my hands spread to the end of the counter, scratching and crawling at the wood. Bracing myself for the impact, the power behind his hard shaft. It was still daylight out, but I didn't give a fuck. If someone wanted to peek in the windows, they'd certainly get one hell of a show.

After Weson had me for a full-course meal, he helped me finish cleaning up, and we headed back to my house. Looking in the rearview mirror, I watched him sing along to a country song in his truck, the light shining in on his bronze face. Shifting my eyes forward, I smiled the rest of the way home. Mesmerized as always by the crisp, golden, and crimson leaves hanging from the trees, the vision of kids picking the amber dandelions in the fields, and the smell of fresh-cut grass flooding into my car. I took it all in and embraced every second. I had everything I ever wanted and was never looking back. Well, unless Weston was behind me, of course.

Arriving home, we were met by Mama and Shadow two. Mom is sitting on the porch swing, just gently rocking back and forth by the tip of her toes. Shadow charged down the steps to greet me, tail wagging and tongue flailing. The sun lowering had spread a glimmer of light across the pond, leaving a crystal shimmer that dazzled. The roses were blushing with vibrant shades of pink, and the sunflowers were brilliantly beaming. My dad would be proud of how beautiful the property looked, that we had horses once again, that mom was happy,  I was safe and back home. Home. The gravel roared behind me, ahh my favorite sound. Turning away from Shadow's playful paws, I watched as my cowboy came down the driveway. My entire life changed in a matter of a few months. One act of bravery, or maybe just being crazy, led me to have my own business, getting my mama back, and bringing the love of my life by my side. A new life, the right life. My life. What was always meant to be? I had gained everything and lost nothing except a bruise or two.

After grilling some Ribeyes and pairing them with sweet corn and cheesy mashed potatoes, we sat around a fire by the pond and drank wine. Even Mama had a glass of wine and told stories of when her and Dad were young. The sun fell, and the moon rose; the stars twinkled above us, and the night sky sparkled. We laughed and talked. Shadow chased fireflies that glowed in the grass, and we watched the flames flicker among the fire. The air became brisk as the wind chilled the evening. Mama said her goodbyes to Weston for the evening and I helped her up from her chair to walk her back to the house.

"I'll be right back, baby. I'll grab more wine, too!" I hollered at Weston as I began walking Mom inside.

Weston gleamed and winked at me, "Hurry back, babe, I'm about ready for dessert."

I blushed and giggled as I escorted mama back to her room and got Shadow settled with her. I scooted my way back to the kitchen and grabbed another bottle of Meiomi Pinot Noir for Weston and I. I yanked a hoodie off the back of the kitchen chair to put it on since it had cooled down outside and made my way towards the front door. Passing through the foyer, I caught my reflection in the mirror that hung on the entry wall. I remember first coming back home to Mama and walking past this same mirror. Not recognizing myself, battered and beaten. Broken and hopeless, scared, swollen, and bruised. A smile began to stretch across my face as I now admired the vision before me. I was happy, healthy, radiant, almost glowing. No more bruises.

Shifting my eyes lower on my body, I noticed something on my arm. I slowly turned to the side to get a better view of the image. Examining myself in the mirror, I realized It was a bruise. A dark, hand-shaped bruise that wrapped around my bicep. It was from Weston. It was from him holding me so tight when he was inside me today, holding me still to have his way with me. Squeezing me so he could go deeper and harder. My grin casting back at me, I couldn't help but think. Maybe a bruise...or two is ok.